Dedicated to the KDa AllStars!

PechaKucha Night

A CELEBRATION

devised and shared by

KLEIN DYTHAM ARCHITECTURE

Pecha Kucha Night, A Celebration; Uleshka Asher Bordini Chikushi, Mark Dytham, Astrid Klein
Printed in Japan

Editor: Uleshka Asher Bordini Chikushi | www.uleshka.com
Copy editor: Selena Hoy
Art direction & design: Ian Lynam | www.ianlynam.com
Illustration: Namaiki | www.namaiki.com
Colophon Typeset in the lovingly handcrafted typeface Auto

20:20 PM:

こんばんは!

(GOOD EVENING!)

A MASSIVE CELEBRATION

When we devised Pecha Kucha Night in Tokyo in February 2003 as a place for young designers to meet, network, and show their work in public, we had no idea of what we were getting ourselves into. About one year ago we had twelve other cities running it, nicely sprinkled across a global map. We got so excited that we just couldn't stop talking about it. Suddenly it turned into a global event happening in close to one hundred cities worldwide, inspiring creative folks on every continent. That made us a little speechless for a moment. Every day we have new people approaching us asking to bring Pecha Kucha to their city as well. Now we think it is time to put out a little statement.

This book is a celebration of Pecha Kucha Night.
It is a line drawn in the sand.
It is a thank you to everyone involved.
It is a statement of our time.

It shows the relevance of real people getting together in a real live situation sharing what they get tinglingly excited about.

We don't know where it will go from here. We wish for it to spread more and allow everyone the opportunity to get out and be inspired. In a few years Pecha Kucha might be a common term found in a dictionary describing a way of making speedy, inspiring presentations.

Who knows?

Whatever happens, we know now that there is a global demand for Pecha Kucha, for a forum in which creative work and thoughts can be easily and informally shown.

If you haven't experienced one yourself, go find a location and join the conversation!

THE DEFINITION OF PECHA KUCHA
from Wikipedia, September 20th 2007

Pecha Kucha (ペチャクチャ) or Pecha Kucha Night is a presentation format in which (mostly creative) work can be easily and informally shown. It was originally devised by Astrid Klein and Mark Dytham of Klein Dytham Architecture (KDa) in Tokyo in 2003 as a place for young designers to meet, network, and show their work in public. The name derives from a Japanese term for the sound of conversation ("chit-chat").

Pecha Kucha (pronounced peh-chak-cha) was started as a designers' show and tell event to attract more people to SuperDeluxe, their multi-media experimental event space they had set up in Roppongi.

The idea behind Pecha Kucha is to keep presentations concise, the interest level up and to have many presenters sharing their ideas within the course of one night. Therefore the 20x20 Pecha Kucha format was created: each presenter is allowed a slideshow of 20 images, each shown for 20 seconds each. This results in a total presentation time of 6 minutes 40 seconds on a stage before the next presenter is up. Each event usually has 14 presenters. Presenters (and much of the audience) are usually from the design, architecture, photography, art and creative fields, but recently it has also stretched over to the business world.

The demand for a place in the city to informally show and share one's work seems to be global - proven by the fact that the event format has been replicated in over 80 cities stretching over every continent, including New York, London, Mexico City, Ljubljana, Bogota, Berlin, Buenos Aires, Tel Aviv, Shanghai, Istanbul and Lagos. Events are usually limited to one each month per city.

Well-known presenters have included the architects Jun Aoki, Toyo Ito, Rem Koolhaas' daughter, designers such as Tom Dixon, Ron Arad, Thomas Heatherwick, comedian Johnny Vegas, actress Joanna Lumley and BBC newscaster Jon Snow. Even Astrid Klein's 5 year old daughter Nanami and Mark Dytham's mother Angela have done presentations in the 20x20 format.

CONCEIVING PECHA KUCHA NIGHT

Conceptions are normally fairly private affairs, but I was present at the moment of the conception of Pecha Kucha Night. I was at Deluxe, interviewing the guys from graphic design firm Namaiki, when Mark Dytham came charging up the stairs into the office. "I f   the space," he said, out of breath – this was the real estate that was to become SuperDeluxe, Pecha Kucha Night's Tokyo womb.

Mark and Astrid Klein of KDa, along with Namaiki, interior design Spinoff, the Nakameguro Yakkyoku record label and the Tokyo Ale brewing company, had set up Deluxe as a loose cooperative of creative firms in 1998. Located in a converted taxi garage, Deluxe occupied what was by Tokyo standards an unusually large space. The various firms had their offices walled off spaces down two sides of the building. A central double-height space was used for meetings or as overflow workspace, but was often made available for performances, workshops, events, and exhibitions. Taking on such a space in the middle of a recession and making it available to the creative community was an act of optimism and generosity. I was interviewing Namaiki's David Duval-Smith and Michael Frank about the vision that had inspired Deluxe. The Deluxe firms were all interested in exploring the zone where the art world, design professions, music and performance disciplines intersected. "There is an area where those things meet," David explained, "from which we can draw out interesting commercial and interesting art projects." As time went by, however, those creative happenings threatened to overwhelm the offices; strolling around an exhibition, you might turn a corner and find yourself in the middle of a staff meeting or a client presentation. They were looking to step up their engineering of creative community another notch, and had set about finding a new space. Namaiki had just finished explaining this when Mark burst into the room. He'd come directly from seeing the big basement loft not far from Deluxe and all its potentials and possibilities were bouncing around in his head.

Deluxe was to be a place that would bring interesting people together and allow them to do interesting things, share thoughts, and exchange ideas. When they shifted their collaborative office events into SuperDeluxe a few years later, Pecha Kucha crystallized all of their intentions and compressed their collaborative, participatory ambitions into a couple of hours. In that moment of conception a potent idea found a fertile space, a connection that eventually led to the birth of Pecha Kucha Night.

Andrew Barrie, PKN Auckland

SCHIEDAM

HOW IT ALL STARTED...

Deluxe, our old shared warehouse office in the middle of Tokyo, is where it all started. Every week we had a design event or an exhibition at the office and we invited some interesting people around. These "open house"- nights were a way to showcase various work in Tokyo but also to develop a vital creative network for us.

When 300 - 400 people tried to squeeze in between our architectural models every week and clients were greeted by an odor of beer and cigarettes the following morning, we decided to move all of the events to a new space: SuperDeluxe! It was big, spacious and had all the opportunities to become the centre of the universe - but it also implied that we had to invent another 20 events to fill up a proper monthly live space schedule. Here is where we needed a good idea!

We had just been to Costa Rica and showed some interesting photos to a small group of people back at our office. Internal "design show and tell" events had always excited us - everything from sharing how we actually make our buildings to holiday snaps. Suddenly it struck us that if we had interesting pictures to talk about, other people must have, too. The question was: how could we make that public and bring it to SuperDeluxe? What could be a possible format that is inviting and inspiring for everyone?

Being architects and having been to countless lectures, we knew that once people start to talk about their work and have a mic in their hands they just go on about details forever. We didn't want a dry lecture from one perspective only. We craved inspirational kicks, sharing many people's thoughts, diverse stories in a casual atmosphere and a chance to talk to both presenters and audience. There needed to be a clear structure, some simple rules set up, a challenge and thrill. After bouncing ideas back and forth we decided to limit the showtime to 20 slides per person projected for 20 seconds each. That kept the presentation time short, but long enough to get the audience excited and to have many people share their thoughts in one night.

About 100 people showed up at our first event in 2003 and it was an instant success. A little dip after the first few rounds helped to firm up the format and find its true rhythm. The amazing thing is that Pecha Kucha Night proves to be fully sustainable: we've been running it every month ever since and enjoy over 300 guests at SuperDeluxe every single time.

UNUSUAL LOCATIONS FOR PECHA KUCHA NIGHT
IF THERE IS NO NOISY HOLE LIKE SUPER DELUXE AVAILABLE IN YOUR CITY,
TRY HOSTING YOUR NEXT PECHA KUCHA IN SOMETHING LIKE ONE OF THESE:

Courtyard of a former police jail (Frankfurt)
Church (Buffalo)
Japanese Embassy (London)
Backyard lawn (Berlin)
Open air amphitheater (New Delhi)
Governmental office tower construction site (Beijing)
Beer garden (New York)
Converted former meat processing plant (Melbourne)
Hotel (Sevilla)
Gas-o-meter of a former gas factory (Amsterdam)
Cantina (Mexico)
Old warehouse at the harbor (Copenhagen)
Art museum (Rotterdam)
100 year old Bathing Club (Trieste)
Cinema (Prague)
Someone's huge loft apartment and their outdoor pool area (Miami)
Theatre (Udine)
Car park (Sydney)
Department store (Gröningen)
Petrol Station (Auckland)

A CULTURAL OUTPOST

Pecha Kucha Night was made to show your work and share your ideas spontaneously and casually without having to chat up a magazine editor, rent an expensive art gallery or endure the stiffness of usual lectures.

Where else can you go if you have just designed a kick-ass dog hair salon - but it's the only project in your portfolio so far? Or your retrospective exhibition finished two months ago but you have a new project to talk about? Or you finished your studies and want to let the city's creatives know that you are hot and available? Or maybe you are visiting and want to check out the colorful potential of that city? Or you came back from an amazing trip and have mind-blowing photos to share?

Until now there simply had been no place in town!

Nova English teacher Chris Silverthorn on his action-packed drawings in Tokyo

A LEVELING EXPERIENCE

If everyone has the same tools to play with, it is revealing how differently people can use them. It is an extremely leveling experience to see a student next to a star designer, having the exact same parameters to work within.

Pecha Kucha works because it is simple and people know exactly what to expect: twenty slides in 6 minutes 40 seconds. This format makes it clear that it is up to the presenter to turn this short slot into a memorable experience.

It equalizes young and old, students and practitioners, amateurs and professionals, creating a playing field that is as egalitarian as it is exciting!

Tokyo was the perfect launch-pad for Pecha Kucha simply because it is a very level playing field in terms of designers. Nobody here has massive egos and there is a much more collaborative feel in the creative scene.

Architects, artists, artisans, breakdancers, comedians, mayors, kids, mums, brain surgeons, human rights watchers, opera singers, students, and star designers have presented next to one another.

Pecha Kucha Night is for everyone and contrasts make the night!

A MORE PERSONALIZED Q&A

When attending lectures, there is usually a short Q&A at the end of a long speech and that's it. Now how many times have you experienced someone occupying the mic for those precious minutes only to hear themselves speak?

Other than a short introduction for every speaker by an energetic host and a short comment after their presentations, there is no official Q&A at Pecha Kucha Night.

Instead the debate happens throughout the entire evening where the audience mingles with the presenters, so the opportunity for actual dialogue is much longer. The casual atmosphere of the room makes it easy to drop all formal barriers and socialize naturally. There are chances to walk up to any presenter either during the presentations, the Beer Break or at the end of Pecha Kucha Night saying "That was fantastic, I love what you do!" - and start a conversation from that.

Like a standard lecture, there is condensed immediate feedback for the presenter right on the stage. Unique to Pecha Kucha Night, however, is the Post Pecha Kucha that follows with extended Q&As around the bar. More than once, this has led to collaborations, employment, and new friends.

FIRST LIFE

Pecha Kucha is a *real* social network. It is the opposite of what happens on the internet where *purported* social networks such as MySpace, Friendster or Mixi make you stay inside behind a tiny screen chatting to an 18 year old girl that is probably an old guy - eventually spending all evening by yourself.

Looking at *only* the images gives one an incomplete understanding of the Pecha Kucha Night experience. The night is all about interaction, direct feedback, eye contact, body heat and excitement - adding that ephemeral, yet essential vehicle which simply cannot be communicated by a computer screen.

People need to talk more and more and extend their knowledge by sharing. Pecha Kucha drags them out from behind their computers into a live situation with atmosphere, energy and real human interaction.

BOGOTA

THE POWER OF 20
There is something amazing about the number 20.

In the beginning we thought that if we invited 20 people to present, they would bring 5 friends each and then we would get about 100 people buying our lovely Tokyo Ale so we would make enough money at the bar to pay the bills. We wanted to start around 8:00 P.M., so that became 20:20. It was a good number for a practical solution that soon sounded like fun. We tried 19 slides or 15 or more, we changed the time, but it never really worked. 20 slides x 20 seconds just seems to be right.

This book was initially planned to have 20 chapters; most of our presentations are based around 20 images - it is simply a good number to get you going.

If you stick to 20, people know what to expect. They sit there and bite their nails anticipating whether the presenter can carry it off or not. Presentations have this final-countdown-game-show-flair to them because the clock keeps ticking in the same rhythm.

Being a little strict with the format has helped Pecha Kucha survive and the Power of 20 is what keeps up the buzz.

GIVING 20X20 TO STUDENTS

Teaching architecture at universities, we realized that most students have no idea of how to present because nobody has actually told them. Most presentations are cluttered, pointless and waste precious time simply because people don't edit their work anymore. There is now infinite storage space on hard disks and digital photography costs nothing once you've got your camera, so we've lost our deleting skills.

This is why the 20x20 format is so important! It forces people to reduce, to clear their minds and think about what is relevant. This doesn't apply to students alone, but when we asked them to present everything to us in Pecha Kucha's 20x20 we were amazed by the difference it made.

They now all start by taking a picture of their site, then a close up of some sketches in their sketchbooks. They find a nice angle and photograph their model - and suddenly students are thinking about the process it takes to design a building!

20x20 is a simple recipe that makes it dead easy for everyone to create a fantastic presentation within half an hour. Now our students have a method to use to explain what their whole project is about in less than seven minutes. Having fifteen minute reviews, there are still another eight minutes left to ask questions and discuss the work with the professors.

It cuts through the crap and gets you going!

LONDON

SUIT & TIE ON SPEED

Pecha Kucha is not only a format that works in the art or design world, but it is one that has been adopted by universities and used as a kick-off for bigger festivals and conferences. Then there are events such as *Pecha Kucha x Design Tide Tokyo* and *Pecha Kucha x Tate Modern,* which show that speed and brevity can add fun, positively contributing to existing brands.

And although Pecha Kucha started off as a creative show and tell event, it has (*drum-roll, please!*) also made its way to the business world and won the hearts of corporations!

Autodesk, the world's biggest developer of architectural software, has licensed the 20x20 format for internal meetings to cut down presentation time and keep their meetings short and informative. RISA Partners (one of Japan's leading real estate and investment firms) thought Pecha Kucha could be just what their company needed to actually get to know each other after their staff increased rapidly. Now they organize a quarterly Corporate Pecha Kucha for the pure purpose of socializing and getting a feel for what is really going on inside RISA. Quite unusual to see SuperDeluxe full of people in suits and ties listening to and making presentations about ghosts, the best places to drink around their office, sky diving, ball room dancing, how to ride a horse to work in Tokyo, and secret maid cafes in Akihabara.

BUENOS AIRES

BERLIN

COPENHAGEN

BANGALORE

PKN GONE VIRAL

Most of the first international Pecha Kucha organizers were presenters at early Tokyo Pecha Kucha Nights and got infected right away. Other people then picked it up in their cities and without any pushing it has spread virally across the world in practically no time. Pecha Kucha is a genuine 100% force-free organic product - but highly contagious!

We have never asked anyone to start or run a Pecha Kucha Night, nor sent out a press release seeking organizers. The formulation of global Pecha Kucha nights has been entirely reliant on word-of-mouth and the internet. Powerful stuff!

In Rotterdam, 350 people queued up outside the Modern Art museum to get into the event. Pecha Kucha went to the ICA in London with 400 people on the waiting list and tickets selling out in less than 20 minutes, making it the fastest selling event in their sixty year history. Melbourne has a regular Pecha Kucha Night with over 1000 guests, and even in places like Bogotá, Colombia it manages to pull together a creative community of around 300 guests every time.

There have been 2973 people at the time of this book's publication who have already presented and we have close to 100 cities in the Pecha Kucha network with new enquiries in our inbox every day.

FROM TOKYO TO BERN, LOS ANGELES, SYDNEY, LONDON, SAN FRANCISCO, STOCKHOLM, ROTTERDAM, GRONINGEN, GLASGOW, BERLIN, SHANGHAI, BUENOS AIRES, HOBART, AMSTERDAM, NEW YORK, OSLO, HELSINKI, BEIJING, PRAGUE, MIAMI, MELBOURNE, TORONTO, VIENNA, BANGKOK, GOTHENBURG, BOGOTA, BANGALORE, UDINE, SAN JOSE, BUFFALO, COLOGNE, MANCHESTER, NEWCASTLE, BELFAST, TAIPEI, SEOUL, AUSTIN,

MARSEILLE, HONG KONG, STUTTGART, SEVILLE, TEL AVIV, FRANKFURT, BUDAPEST, AUCKLAND, LISBON, SEATTLE, LJUBLJANA, MONTREAL, COPENHAGEN, WASHINGTON DC, SAO PAULO, HAMBURG, EDINBURGH, KUALA LUMPUR, PORTE ALEGRE, MADRID, CHICAGO, SEATTLE, LINZ, LIMA, ATLANTA, BRUSSELS, HARVARD, KAMPALA UGANDA, LAGOS, PERTH, PARIS, PORTLAND, RIGA, ROTTERDAM, SANTIAGO, SCHIEDAM, TREVISO, VIENNA, WELLINGTON...

PRESENTATION

There are 31 presentations in this book. A teeny weeny cross-section just to give you a small taste of the variety shown at Pecha Kucha Nights around the planet. Nice, but far away from the real thing! The slides are the basis for conversation and the 20x20 format pulls it all together, but Pecha Kucha Night is really about the people and the adrenaline in the air.

Toyo Ito made the audience crack up talking about the pitches he has lost against Rem Koolhaas. Sebastian Conran showed the cover he designed for The Clash, but what do you think is this strange Michelin man on a church window about? Are those traditionally-pimped-out Japanese cars seriously hearses? And why would anyone collect the exact same record 20 times? What the hell are those presenters actually talking about? These kinds of questions ensure that the room is constantly abuzz with discussion and debate.

When checking the presenters' slides on a computer before the actual event, they often look like they could be the most boring presentations ever. But on the night itself, the crowd is waiting, the room is dark and steamy, the slides come up, and the presenter approaches the stage... Sweaty hands clutch a microphone and suddenly there is magic! It is the people – not just the work - that make the night, the stories pouring out of them and the waves of excitement flooding the room.

Nonetheless, here are 31 presentations which show the breadth of subjects and the variety or presentations. These will never make up for the live presentation. They are just a visual hint of what you have missed!

GUERILLA GARDENERS

Presenter: Namaiki
City: Tokyo Vol 46
Date: 15 October 2007
Guests: 390
Topic: More Green!

"THE BEAUTY OF PECHA KUCHA IS THAT IT SEEMS TO UNLEASH ENERGY AND GOODWILL IN EQUAL MEASURE. FAMOUS PEOPLE AND NOT-YET-FAMOUS PEOPLE JUMP AT THE OPPORTUNITY TO TAKE PART. EVEN EXPERIENCED PRESENTERS WORK INCREDIBLY HARD TO PREPARE THEIR PIECE. AND CELEBRITY EGOS SEEM TO DISAPPEAR, AS IF BY MAGIC, ON THE NIGHT ITSELF.
LONG LIVE PECHA KUCHA!"

JOHN THACKARA, DESIGN GURU, CRITIC AND BUSINESS PROVOCATEUR

A COLLECTOR

Presenter: Shinobu Machida
City: Tokyo Vol 19
Date: 26 January 2005
Guests: 380
Topic: A collection of Japanese Hearses

In this, the "golden age" of the funeral coach, the carved reached its peak of ornamentation and ostentation. This

BODY BUILT BY A. GEISSEL & SONS, PHILA. PA.

画像無断転載禁止

画像無断転載禁止

画像無断転載禁止

画像無断転載禁止

画像無断転載禁止

画像無断転載禁止

画像無断転載禁止

画像無断転載禁止

画像無断転載禁止

"DOING YOUR FIRST PECHA KUCHA PRESENTATION IS VERY MUCH LIKE THE FIRST TIME YOU HAVE SEX. YOU WILL BE CRIPPLINGLY NERVOUS, YOUR TIMING IS ALL WRONG AND YOU HAVE LITTLE IDEA OF WHEN IT'S GOING TO END."

YONGFOOK, WEB PRODUCER

EMBROIDERERS

Presenter: Martin Bricelj
City & Vol: Ljubljana Vol 1
Date: 5 April 2007
Guests: 200
Topic: Pornogobelin

"The well tested recipe for bursts of laughter!"

HELLO
WORLD!

Draw your gobelin and order the embroidered version from us!   EMBROIDER

PORNO
GOBELIN
D.I.Y. KIT

Creez-vous votre gobelin!

VKLJUČUJE:
-PREDTISKANI STRAMIN
-16 KLOPČIČEV GARNA
-ŠIVANKO
-POSTER

Naredi svoj gobelin!

25x35cm

pornogobelin.com

Tomoko Azumi unfolding her creations at Pecha Kucha Tokyo Vol.20

AN ARCHITECT

Presenter: Toyo Ito
City:Tokyo Vol 7
Date: 24 September 2003
Guests: 260
Topic: Series of unknown projects: Architecture
and furniture

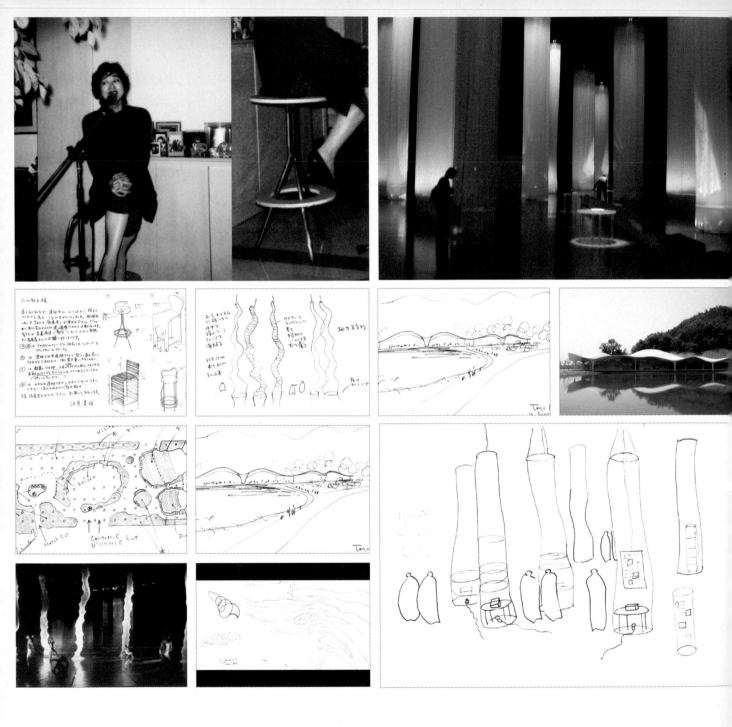

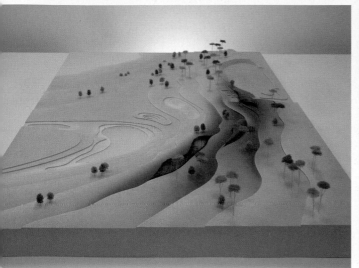

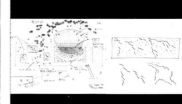
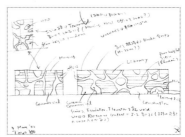
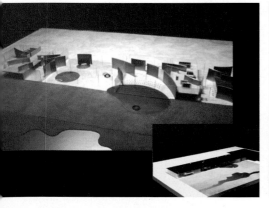
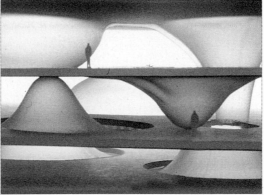

Structural Void System

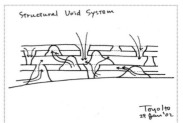

Toyo Ito
29 Jan '02

"BOGOTÁ IS A COLD, SHAPE-SHIFTING, PASSIVE-AGGRESSIVE AND SURPRISING BEAST OF A CITY. DECIDEDLY NOT SPECTACULAR, ITS REAL CHARM LIES PRECISELY ON THIS BEING NON-SPECTACULAR. BOGOTÁ IS OBLIVIOUS TO ITS OWN BEAUTY, AND IT'S ALL THE BETTER FOR IT, BOGOTÁ IS FULL OF SECRETS YOU'VE GOT TO DISCOVER. IN THAT SENSE, PKN IN BOGOTÁ ACQUIRES A NEW MEANING, AS FOR ONE NIGHT IT MAKES THE BEAST EXPOSE A FEW OF ITS MANY SECRET TALENTS, BRINGING TOGETHER THE HEARTS AND MINDS OF MANY CURIOUS BOGOTOKIANS! THANK YOU!"

ALEJANDRO Z. AND NOBARA HAYAKAWA FROM PKN BOGOTA

DESIGN RESEARCHERS

Presenter: Popular de Lujo
City: Bogotá Vol 2
Date: 1 March 2007
Guests: 400
Topic: Vernacular visual communication and popular culture in Bogotá and other Latin American cities

"Through 5 years of relentless work, the Popular de Lujo collective (Juan Esteban Duque, Esteban Ucrós) has achieved a massive reputation as one of the fiercest tribes of visual hunters/gatherers in the wild visual jungle that is Bogotá. Professional graphic designers by trade, they have tuned their senses to discover the richness, ingenuity and effectiveness of the graphic language that comes from the real people in the streets, and have set out to document its influence and legacy in the mainstream and underground culture."

«BOGOTÁ, TAN HORRIBLE COMO SIEMPRE.»
— WILLIAM BURROUGHS

...un BESO para BOGOTA EN SUS 466 AÑOS

DIVERSOS ÁNGULOS

ESPÍRITU COOPERATIVO

STICKERS LEGENDARIOS

I ♥ mi Bus

APROX. 150 PERSONAS INVOLUCRADAS

FRANCIA EN LA CULTURA BOGOTANA

POPULARDELUJO

Refrescos del Pais y de Latas

Cristo te ama

GRÁFICA CALLEJERA BORICUA

MOVIE STARS ENTRE NOSOTROS

"HOW DO YOU GET A BUNCH OF VISUAL VISIONARIES-MANY OF THEM ISOLATED, INTROVERTED, SELF-EMPLOYED PEOPLE WHO TEND TO HUNCH ALL DAY BEHIND THEIR COMPUTERS – OUT INTO A LIVE SPACE, COMMUNICATING, DRINKING, NETWORKING?

THE SOLUTION: GIVE THEM A FORMAT, A STRUCTURE, A PARLOR GAME, A CHANCE TO TALK ABOUT THEIR CURRENT INTERESTS AND LISTEN TO OTHERS DOING THE SAME."

MOMUS, WIRED

A TRAVELING CRAFTSMAN

Presenter: Max Lamb
City: Design Tide 2006 Pecha Kucha Night
Date: 3 November 2006
Guests: 430
Topic: Design experiments with local craftspeople
and local, traditional materials

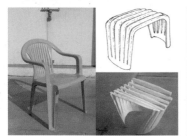

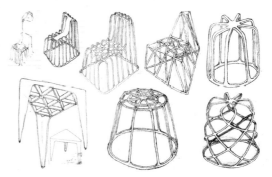

ASSORTED FLAVORS OF PECHA KUCHA

One of the most amazing things about Pecha Kucha is *surprise*.

We organized an internal, corporate Pecha Kucha in Las Vegas last year for Autodesk, a huge world renowned software company and we had a room full of hard core Autodesk users and developers. We managed to persuade the CEO Carl Bass to do a Pecha Kucha presentation and he just laid it all out there. Carl talked about being into carpentry when he was really young, and what I didn't know even after working with him for 10 years is that he is a fine carpenter.

When he showed a slide of himself - standing there with a huge afro - with a house he had built on a native Indian reservation in South Dakota in his 20s, I swear that everybody in the room had a different understanding of both Carl and that company.

Pecha Kucha seems to work for many different occasions. We introduced it to Harvard as part of the great Alumni week in 2006. Graduate students from the last 50 years of Harvard came, so there was a really wide range of old practitioners and great young students. There were also lots of other people from the San Francisco Bay and Boston areas so Pecha Kucha just seemed like the perfect format for the community to get to know itself.

Now Pecha Kucha will be hosted at Harvard twice a year. It will be for students but also open for people at other schools and the general professional Boston community. This really establishes the university as a hub and expands its role beyond that of a student body. One special thing about Pecha Kucha is that at its core it stays Pecha Kucha, but it takes on totally different personalities depending on the context and the city it is in. I have been to Pecha Kucha Nights in Tokyo, recently presented in Berlin, and I organize the ones in San Francisco, Las Vegas, and Harvard and helped set them up in Seattle. They are all unique.

Berlin for example had this total gritty, intellectual Berlin feeling to it. It couldn't have been anywhere else in the world, but again the magic of Pecha Kucha just worked - the way it always does.

Paul Jamtgaard, Pecha Kucha San Francisco

AN ARCHITECT

Presenter: Mark Dytham
City: Tokyo Vol 4
Date: 25 June 2003
Guests: 140
Topic: Pigeon race in Poole, England

from the existing lifting bridge of new
shore observation pier showing boathouse
ed below and west side public space in the
ground

new along new stretch
showing relationship to
buildings, pavement areas
and street furniture

section and part plan of new
showing relationship with

Last Updated: Saturday, 21 June, 2003, 21:48 GMT 22:48 UK

E-mail this to a friend   Printable version

Pigeons boost tennis game

Africa
Americas
Asia-Pacific
Europe
Middle East
South Asia
UK
Business
Health
Science/Nature
Technology
Entertainment
Have Your Say
Country Profiles
In Depth
Programmes

Pigeons are as much a part of Wimbledon as strawberries and cream but this year they may well be carrying a special message for tennis fans.

Acclaim, publishers of a video tennis game designed for PlayStation2, will be releasing specially trained homing pigeons, emblazoned with the game's logo.

Spray-painted pigeons are advertising Virtua Tennis 2

Twenty birds will be spray-painted with the Virtua Tennis 2 logo and trained to fly in and out of the home of British tennis during the 2003 Wimbledon championships which start next week.

The novel marketing ploy is guaranteed to get both tennis and bird fans in a flap.

RELATED SITES
BBC SPORT

Flying billboard

SEE ALSO:
Tim's mothe...
13 Jun 03 |
Seaweed re...
04 Jun 03 |
Gangster vid...
02 Jun 03 |
Angelina 'br...
03 Jul 01 |
Nude volley...
makers
01 Apr 03 |
Games indu...
09 Jan 03 |
Video games...
28 May 03 |

RELATED INTE...
Acclaim
Wimbledon C...
The BBC is n...
content of ext...

TOP TECHNO...
Acclaim sells it
Weird web d...

"SAY WHAT YOU NEED TO SAY IN SIX MINUTES AND 40 SECONDS OF EXQUISITELY MATCHED WORDS AND IMAGES AND THEN SIT THE HELL DOWN. THE RESULT, IN THE HANDS OF MASTERS OF THE FORM, COMBINES BUSINESS MEETING AND POETRY SLAM TO TRANSFORM CORPORATE CLICHE INTO SURPRISINGLY COMPELLING BEAT-THE-CLOCK PERFORMANCE ART."

DANIEL H. PINK, WIRED

A DESIGNER

Presenter: Sebastian Conran
City: Design UK 2005 Pecha Kucha Night Tokyo
Date: 31 October 2005
Guests: 450
Topic: His family, his first design pieces, his cars
and things that inspire him

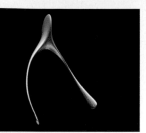

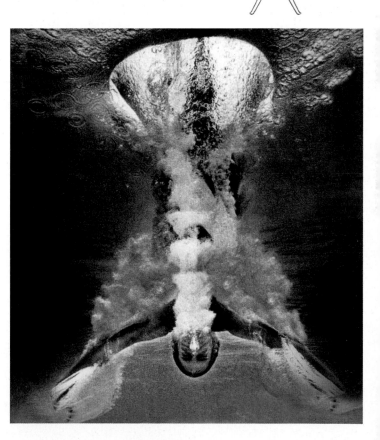

IT'S ALL IN THE MIX

Usually, events in Buenos Aires are restricted to one discipline only. On top of that, people tend to get even more specialized: they don't only have a profession, but a master's degree or Ph.D. specializing within that profession. I always wanted to bring different creative people together and see how they would react and inspire each other. Essentially that is what Pecha Kucha enables you to do: mix!

Different disciplines, males and females, students and experts, and particularly old and young come together at Pecha Kucha. We had DaniDan, an 18 year old artist presenting right before Justo Solsona, 75 year old established architect who still builds airports around the world. They fell in love with each other! The young one was amazed at this guy who still builds big things at 75. And the old one was astonished at the 18 year old who has so much to show already and knows what he wants to do in life.

It's really rewarding and important in a country with a history full of so much pain – economically and politically - that has caused whole generations to be cut off from each other.

We also bring old traditional craftsmen with disappearing skills to present at Pecha Kucha to inspire the young. Imagine how much a graphic design student can learn from a guy who uses nothing but a pencil! Or we include "distant professions" such as chefs or biologists to bring out their creative side as well.

Argentina is a very big country and some people have actually spent more than 10 hours on the bus and traveled over 600 kilometers for their 6 minutes 40 seconds. It is that important to them!

I thought people would like to be part of something international at first, but it soon became so established that I didn't feel the need to mention all the other cities anymore. In fact, when I first said it was international, there were only 7 other Pecha Kucha cities. Now that I don't say it anymore there are 100!

The other day when I read 'Lagos' on the list of cities, I actually had to look it up to find out in which country it was - and I live in Argentina, which is quite unknown as well. Knowing that there are people in Nigeria gathering for Pecha Kucha makes them family somehow, although I have never been there. What that means is that this event can be completely local, but you still feel strongly connected to all the other cities in the network. I hope that we will all be able to "swap" presenters in the future to exchange even more than we already do. Pecha Kucha really mixes up everything and everyone. It seems to find a way to bring people together who never even thought of meeting each other. That is the beauty of it.

May Groppo, PKN Buenos Aires

AN ILLUSTRATOR

Presenter: Mónica Naranjo
City: Bogotá Vol 3
Date: 28 June 2007
Guests: 500
Topic: A thorough retrospective of paintings, comics, photographs and animations

"From the city of Medellín, the uber-talented Mónica Naranjo mesmerised the audience with her creative work that through a seemingly restrained approach to colour, form and composition, manages to evoke the sublime and the mundane surrounding everyday. At the end of her presentation we were left wondering why life was so unfair by granting Mónica a vision that can see through to the bare soul of things whereas the rest of us are only granted with eyeballs?"

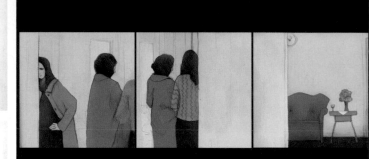

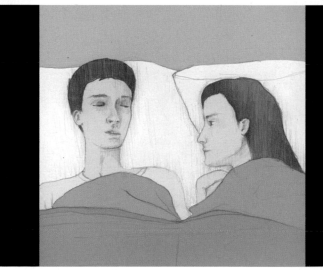

this is our last goodbye

"I'M NOT SURE I UNDERSTAND JUST WHY, BUT THE PECHA KUCHA FORMAT SEEMS TO HAVE A NATURAL AFFINITY THAT BRINGS OUT THE PASSION IN PRESENTERS. IT SEEMS TO BE ESPECIALLY EFFECTIVE FOR THOSE WHO RARELY MAKE PRESENTATIONS OR SPEAK UP OR WHO DON'T THINK THEY HAVE MUCH TO CONTRIBUTE. PECHA KUCHA HELPS THEM FIND THEIR "VOICE" AND ACTS AS A VEHICLE FOR TRANSPORTING THEIR MESSAGE TO OTHERS. POWERFUL STUFF!"

WAYNE HODGINS, OFF COURSE ON TARGET, STRATEGIC FUTURIST AUTODESK INC.

AN ENGINEER

Presenter: Ugo Conti
City: Las Vegas Vol 1
Date: 1 November 2006
Guests: 300
Topic: My life as an Engineer: An Ocean Journey

"Ugo's calm delivery completely belied the
truly innovative approach to an ancient design
problem. He blew everyone in the room away."

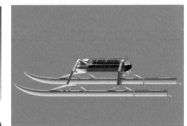

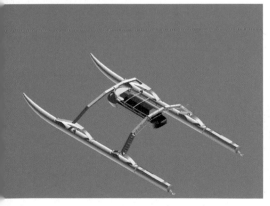

Stay Tuned...

"*IF YOU COULD MAKE A COCKTAIL TO MATCH THE FLAVOUR OF THE EVENING IT MIGHT JUST BE RHUBARB CRUMBLE VODKA: SURPRISING, UNIQUE, COLOURFUL AND SURE TO GET YOUR HEAD SPINNING WITH ONE GULP!*"

EMER MCCOURT, DOTT07

A PUBLISHER

Presenter: Thomas Jeppe
City: Melbourne Vol 1
Date: September 24th, 2003
Guests: 700
Topic: Home-made Tattoos Rule

Thomas Jeppe stole the show at Pecha Kucha Melbourne Vol 1. He's a young guy
who is so passionate about hand-done tattoos that he published a book which
featured his friends' tattoos, his own, and all of the stuff that inspires them to keep
on adding to their amazing human canvases. It was at once hilarious, serious and
informative, and more like 'slap you in the face' stand-up comedy that we have ever
featured at PK Night in Melbourne. After staging 4 volumes of Pecha Kucha Night in
Melbourne so far, with 500-1000 people attending each one, people still remember
Thomas Jeppe as one of the most outstanding and unique presenter they have seen.
He energized, entertained and educated the crowd.

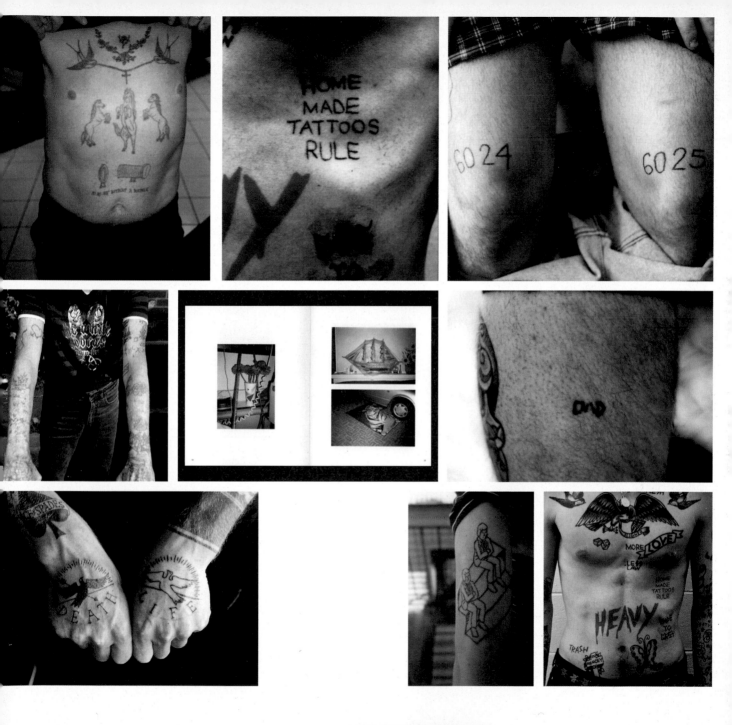

Nanami on her drawings in Tokyo

A DAUGHTER

Presenter: Nanami
City: Tokyo Vol 35
Date: 9 August 2006
Guests: 410
Topic: The Natural History Museum in London,
her drawings and sculptures

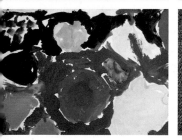

"NOT EXCLUSIVE, BUT INCLUSIVE. PECHA KUCHA NIGHT IS THE REVERSE OF THE '50S EXPERT CULTURE WHERE YOU ARE FORCED TO ACCEPT EXCLUSIVE OPINIONS ON HOW THINGS ARE SUPPOSED TO BE. THE NEW TIME AND CULTURE IS ALL ABOUT INCLUSIVENESS, INTEGRATING AS MANY PEOPLE FROM AS MANY DIFFERENT BACKGROUNDS AS POSSIBLE. IT INVOLVES THE PEOPLE IT IS FOR."

ANA PINTO DA SILVA, PKN SEATTLE

A PRODUCT DESIGNER

Presenter: Hironao Tsuboi
City: Tokyo Vol 43
Date: 27 June 2007
Guests: 360
Topic: His design work

Hironao Tsuboi

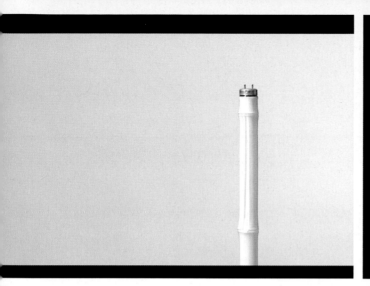

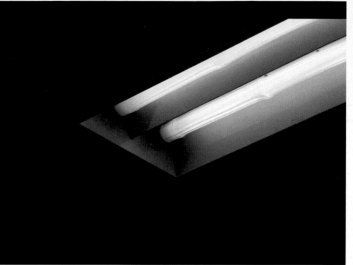

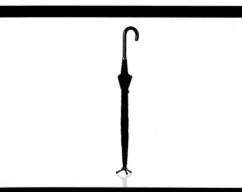

Thank you very much for your attention.

Angela Dytham presenting at Pecha Kucha Tokyo Vol. 13

A MOTHER

Presenter: Angela Dytham
City: Tokyo Vol 13
Date: 28 April 2004
Guests: 280
Topic: Her creations: her children, floral
arrangements, and wedding cakes

UDINE?

When we saw the list of some 40 cities where Pecha Kucha already existed, including New York, Beijing, Shanghai, London, Berlin, Amsterdam and Buenos Aires, we were doubtful whether such a metropolitan thing could function in a city with less than 100,000 inhabitants and a fame for inactivity - like Udine!

With Udine, at that time by far the smallest Pecha Kucha city and us being rather inexperienced event organizers, we were told by locals that "you should be happy if 60 people show up!" We responded that we would not be happy at all if only 60 attended, but our knees were shaking a bit when we said it. Because of these estimates, we chose a bar with a maximum seating capacity of 100, so the place wouldn't look too empty.

For a combination of reasons we had to organize the evening on a cold February Monday - probably the worst evening of the week to organize any kind of event. Of course it was raining cats, dogs, and elephants as well, and when we arrived at the cultural centre we found out that there were actually two other important cultural events going on starting half an hour before our Pecha Kucha Night. With absolutely no parking for some kilometers, how many Italians would join us for a strange phenomenon with an unpronounceable name organized by two people not particularly known to important-in-crowd-personalities in Udine?

We were happy when the first guests started coming and super-surprised to see the space slowly filling up and - eventually - even getting full! When the space got unbelievably busy, people continued to stand outside in their raincoats under a small awning. Pushing each other in and trying not to get too wet, they followed the presentations by looking through the windows. At a certain point we really had to close the door, because 300 people had entered and the owner of the bar started to be afraid that something might happen to the relatively fragile construction on which his old building rested. By the end of the evening we had sent about 130 more guests home who had really wanted to attend!

This Pecha Kucha in a really small provincial city also included a presentation by one of the youngest participants ever. My daughter, 8 years old, had seen us preparing, talking, and discussing, and so she became really enthusiastic and wanted to be a part of the organization. After trying really hard, she realized that 20 drawings were a bit tough to prepare, but she wanted to present *something*. And so in the end I was really surprised to find my 8 years old daughter completely at ease with the mic saying her few lines of introduction to a room bursting with people.

Big girl, I thought. Big girl, big Pecha Kucha on a cold and rainy evening in a small provincial town - that for one night shared a rather metropolitan atmosphere.

Mirko Van Den Winkel

AN ARTIST

Presenter: James Newitt
City: Hobart Vol 2
Date: 30 August 2006
Guests: 70
Topic: Real Fictions

"James' work reveals aspects of human nature,
dialogue and place that are unspoken or
simmering under the surface of the human
condition. Drawing parallels between disjointed
communities and individuals, the narratives that
emerge are both touching and confronting."

These kids have been child soldiers you know, walking around in the army with machine guns, and killing people. And then they come to Hobart and all of a sudden teachers are like 'don't wear sneakers, do your laces up'.

Imagine having lived through that and then someone's telling you to tuck your shirt in.

I was on my bike, and he cleaned me up.

I've got a new friend now. She's very loud though. She doesn't mean to be. I keep on saying to her "shut up we're talking about little soft things."

In my cell at night I think about that.

My daughter turns thirteen this year and I don't ever want her to touch drugs. I don't ever want her to sleep with people just to feel wanted.

Yes, I was a dancing teacher all my life. My hobby was always the tap dancing, but I worked for many, many years in the lottery office as an ordinary clerk.

I was never ordinary.

Australian Posters

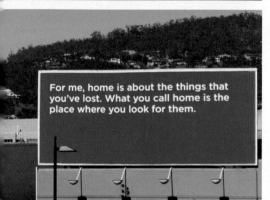

Art performance by Willem van Hest and Ron Blom explaining
how they work together, Pecha Kucha Rotterdam Vol. 6

A GRAPHIC DESIGNER

Presenter: C. Diego LAB
City: San Jose, Costa Rica
Date: 10 May 2007
Guests: 220
Topic: Amazingly colorful 3D graphics

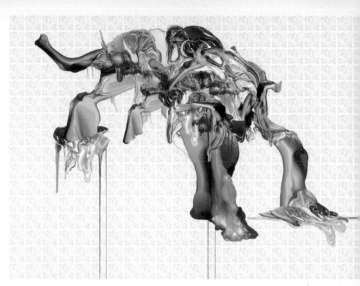

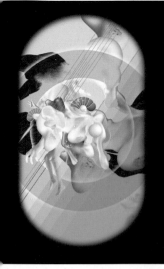
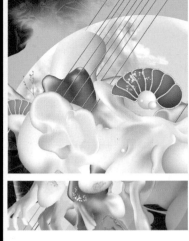

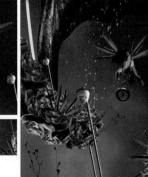

BIENVENIDOS

✶SALON DE BANQUETES✶
"COVADONGA
RESERVACIONES 55 33 29 22
55 33 27 01
PB CANTINA
CHAMELO-PECHA KUCHA
LA CAVA

1ER° PISO-RESTAURANTE
G-1
G-2
G-3
G-4

HAW-
2PISO-SALON CANTABRICO

A wonderful welcome at Salon Covadonga! The official signage for
Pecha Kucha held in an old cantina in Mexico City.

A DESIGNER

Presenter: Jens Thomas
City: Göteborg Vol 1
Date: 6 December 2006
Guests: 100
Topic: Ice hotel - A life story

"Jens' Pecha Kucha is a life story about water. At a certain moment the water of Torne River turns into ice. This process has the perfect speed to develop totally clear ice. He wanted to show what he can do while the water is in its frozen state. The story shows three different concepts. First working with ice in cold environment outdoors (Ice hotel). Then in a warm environment outdoors and indoors. And finally in a cold but artificial environment. The life story ends with the ice melting back into water. The life circle can now start over again."

"WITH AN ECLECTIC MIXTURE OF SPEAKERS AND FAMOUS NAMES APPEARING BACK TO BACK WITH COMPLETE UNKNOWNS, THE CONTRAST WITH THE TRADITIONAL LECTURE COULD NOT BE GREATER."

ICON JUNE 2006

A TYPOGRAPHER

Presenter: Odod Ezer
City: Tel Aviv Vol 1
Date: 1 August 2007
Guests: 300
Topic: Commercial and experimental Typographic works

"Oded's presentation was a fascinating display of his passion
for letters, especially Hebrew ones. In his experimental
work, boundaries between art and typography were blurred,
and the result was impressive, poetic and even funny.You can
imagine the audience was completely mesmerized…"

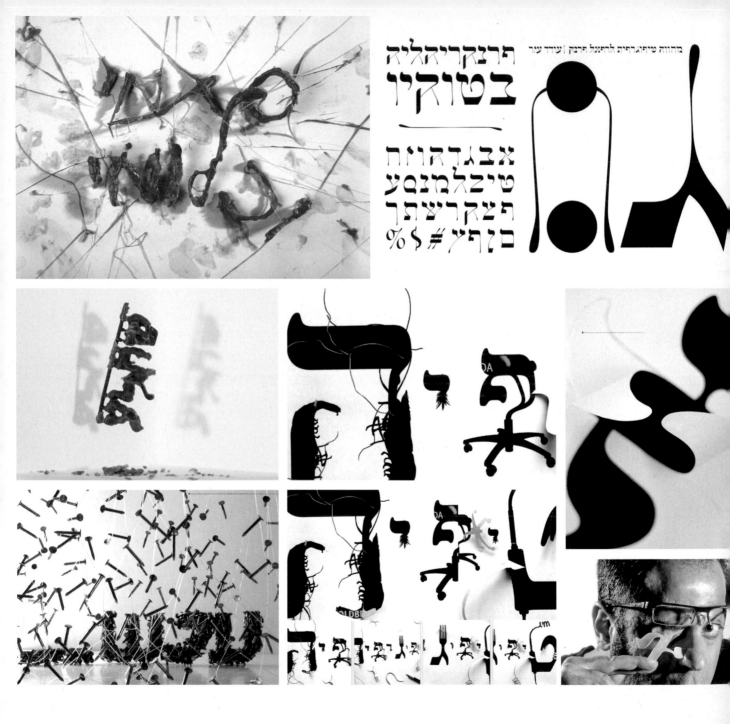

מהדורה סידורית רחבה לרחיאל ארבק | עודד עזר

תרנקריאליה
בטוקיו
—
אבגדהוזח
טיכלמנסע
פצקריצתר
ן ת ף ץ # $ %

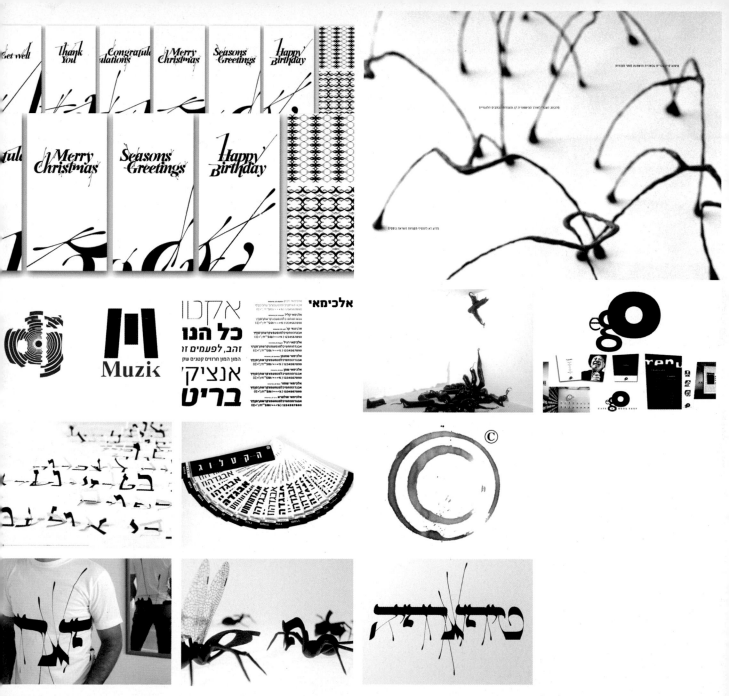

"TELL ME A PROBLEM THAT CAN'T BE OUTLINED IN 6 MINUTES AND 40 SECONDS AND I'LL SHOW YOU A PROBLEM THAT'S PROBABLY NOT WORTH HAVING A MEETING ABOUT."

SETH GODIN, AUTHOR: AGENT OF CHANGE

AN ARCHITECT

Presenter: Astrid Klein
City: Tokyo Vol 40
Date: 27 March 2007

Guests: 370
Topic: My flower pots

PECHA KUCHA GOES ORANJE OR HOW AN ENTIRE COUNTRY WENT PECHA KUCHA CRAZY

For the first Pecha Kucha in Holland, we hired a space underneath the cinema Cinerama in Rotterdam and invited friends and colleagues to give presentations. We sent out the buzz in the city that the first Pecha Kucha Night was coming soon and the place was so packed that we had to send eighty more people away.

The success of the first night didn't go unnoticed and within a week we received thirteen requests from all over the Netherlands asking leave to organize Pecha Kucha Nights as well. This completely shocked us because when we started, Rotterdam was the sixth city outside Tokyo with a Pecha Kucha Night. If all these requests were granted there would be nine Dutch cities with Pecha Kucha Nights and three in Amsterdam alone - in a country no bigger than Tokyo Prefecture!

Still, almost weekly we receive these requests. In total we have been approached by eighteen different cities (we believe there actually aren't any more cities in The Netherlands!) and in some cities by up to seven different parties.

At the first Pecha Kucha Night in Rotterdam, a curator of Boijmans Van Beuningen (the best art museum in the country), was in the audience and got so excited that she invited us to have the second Pecha Kucha Night at the museum. This resulted in a memorable evening for Rotterdam with a queue in front of the museum that had never been so long.

The Pecha Kucha Night in the museum was held surrounded by priceless paintings of Dutch masters. Only a thin rope in front of the paintings separated the beer-drinking crowd from these treasures. This was the kickoff for many crazy Pecha Kucha Nights to follow in Rotterdam!

Bart Cardinaal, PKN Rotterdam

DESIGNERS

Presenter: Mario Minale and Kuniko Maeda
City: Rotterdam Vol 4
Date: August 2006
Guests: 250
Topic: Food design

"They gave a whole new meaning to
toasted bread."

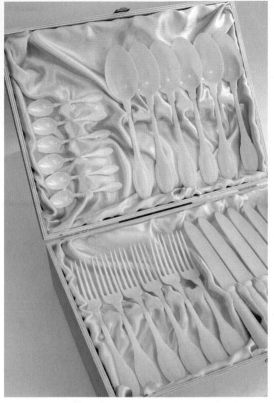

Thomas Heatherwick and his grandmother at London's Pecha Kucha in Sadler's Wells

A RESEARCHER

Presenter: Archana Prasad
City: Bangalore Vol 2
Date: 26 April 2007
Guests: 550
Topic: Iron Lattice Flowers - her diaries

"Archana's rhetorical style is expressed in two complementary idioms - lyrical drawing and painterly words. And each speaks to the other in her on-going documentation of a fascinating persona inspired by her own life's wanderings and wonderings. Her debut of these works at the CKS Courtyard for PKN Bangalore 2 brought the house down.

Being a researcher for Microsoft, it was the first time for her to show drawings and perform poetry. Archana's Pecha Kucha experience strengthened her decision to quit her job and follow her heart into the world of poetry, art and performance..."

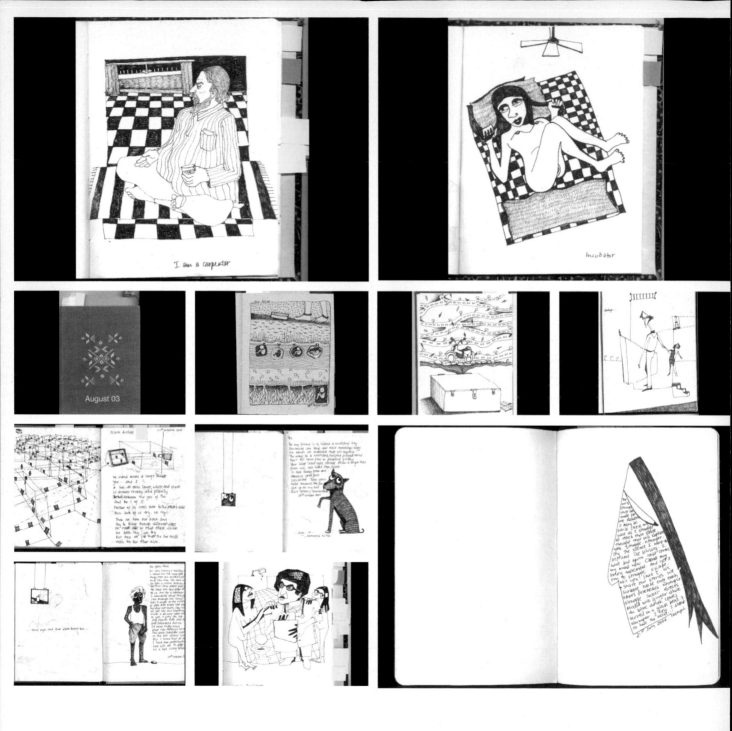

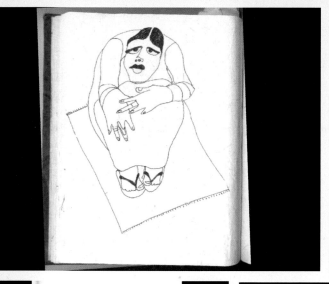

AN ORGANIZER'S MIRACLE!

Setting up Pecha Kucha Berlin was already mind-blowing, but as an organizer Auckland topped Berlin.

The first Pecha Kucha Night Auckland wasn't planned - it just happened. I arrived back in Auckland in April 2007 and thought about setting up a Pecha Kucha test version at some point in the distant future just like we did in Berlin to see how people here would react to it. That was when I got an email from Mark Dytham saying that he would be in Auckland at the end of April and would like to kick off the first Pecha Kucha Night in New Zealand right away. Heart attack! One week to organize an event which should be big - but most Kiwis had never heard about Pecha Kucha Night. Plus I hadn't been back to New Zealand for five years, so that was that for my creative network. Luckily, the website in Berlin was all set up (thanks, Joachim Stein!) which helped to give me some Pecha Kucha credibility.

A fruitful local collaboration with architect Andrew Barrie also helped to get things moving. Countless phone calls explaining Pecha Kucha, mountains of Fwd:Fwd:Fwd:- emails and 6 days of sweat got us there. Finally we had a wonderful location and 11 speakers lined up. Kiwis are very hesitant about new movements but the simplicity of the format won: 320 real people were sitting in front of a big screen waiting for the very first Pecha Kucha Night in New Zealand to begin.

Mark started with the first presentation and the room went totally quiet. New Zealand had never seen anything like this before. Totally different from what I was used to in Berlin, where people have high-class, creative events at every corner and audiences are hard to excite - the atmosphere in Auckland was as if the first ship had just arrived.

As an organizer, this was incredibly rewarding - and fun. New Zealand really needs events like this! There are so many interesting stories to tell and amazing pictures to be shown. Kiwis are hard to get in front of a microphone but once there, they love to talk.

Luka Hinse, PKN Auckland

AN ARCHITECT

Presenter: Peter Exley
City: Chicago Vol 1
Date: 29 May 2007
Guests: 200
Topic: Taking children seriously, and respecting
their ideas and ideals.

"Children are sophisticated, have strong opinions, and have very
good taste. They enjoy art. It's often the adults in their lives
that don't know how to appreciate art and beauty anymore.
Viva grubbiness, risk, challenge, mischief, play and fun. Thanks
to Peter for encouraging kids and reminding adults!"

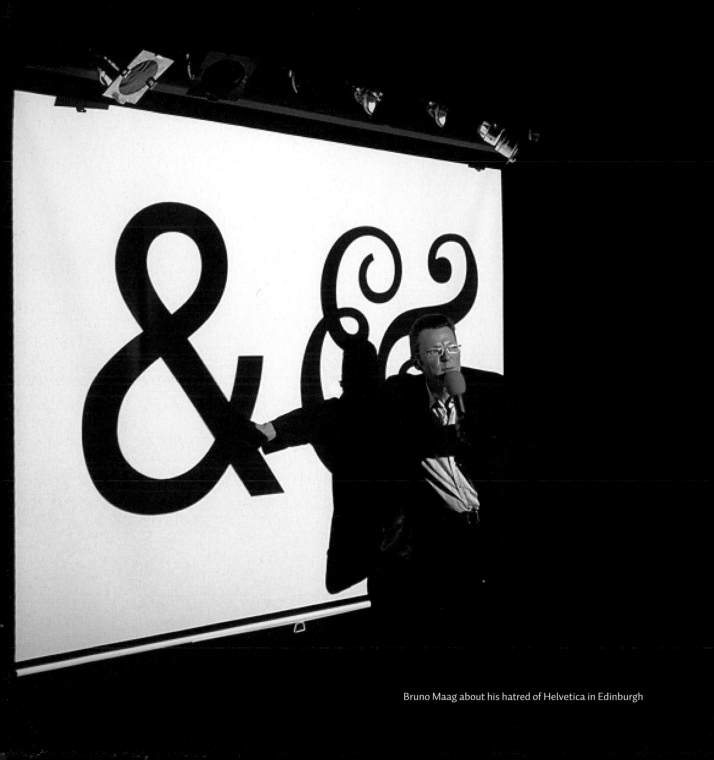

Bruno Maag about his hatred of Helvetica in Edinburgh

A DESIGN JOURNALIST

Presenter: Marcus Fairs
City: Glasgow Vol 1
Date: 30 March 2006
Guests: 250
Topic: How all of his "designed" furniture is
actually flawed, with the exception of his loyal
£2.99 IKEA lamp

A CITY MAYOR

Presenter: Mayor David Miller
City & Vol: Toronto Vol 1
Date: 25 May 2007
Guests: 550
Topic: Visions for Toronto seen through the eyes
of the city's photo bloggers

The Michael Lee-Chin Crystal Opens June 2007

"YOU CAN JUST GO TO GRAZE OTHER PEOPLE'S THOUGHTS. IF YOU'RE INTO SOMETHING YOU CAN GO AND TALK TO THEM AFTERWARDS. IF NOT, IT'S ONLY A SHORT SHARP PAIN TO LISTEN TO THEM."

DAMIEN BARR, THE TIMES (UK)

AN ARTIST

Presenter: Bruno 9li
City: Porto Alegre Vol 1
Date: 27 May 2007
Guests: 250
Topic: Showcase of Bruno 9li's works from the
past few years.

"Pretty powerful imagery, inspired by oriental
flavors and alchemy."

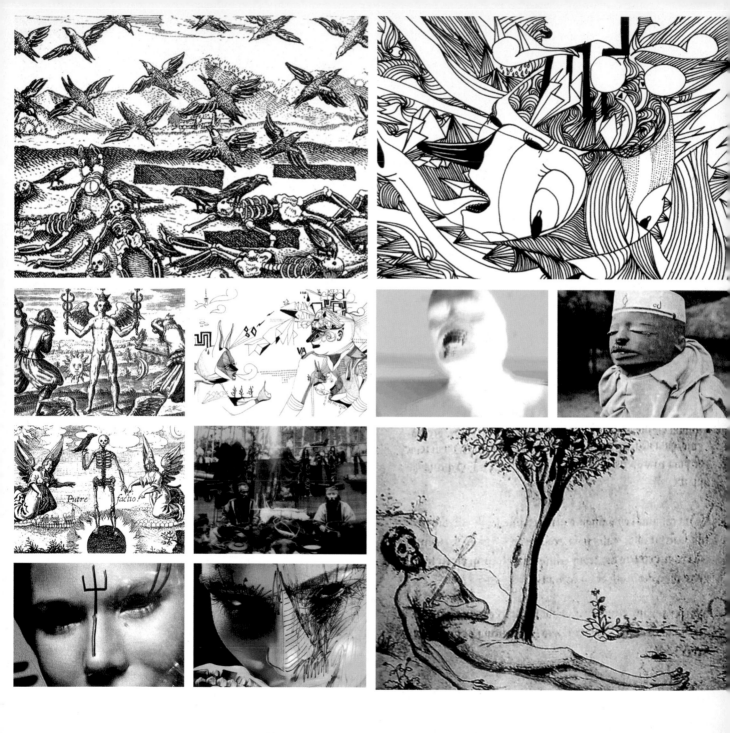

Schlitzi and Murli from Club Real presenting their Finland holiday
snaps at Pecha Kucha Berlin

A PHOTOGRAPHER

Presenter: Eric Leleu
City: Shanghai Vol 5
Date: 25 February 2007
Guests: 320
Topic: Photography about people sleeping in public in China

"His mix of music and images make his works come alive, the two parts of his presentation (slow/fast) created a great contrast."

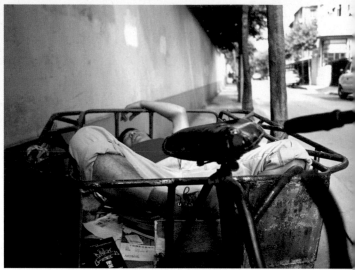

Long queue outside the Boijmans Van Beuningen art museum for Pecha Kucha Rotterdam Vol.2

A PERFORMER

Presenter: William Willems
City: Amsterdam Vol 1
Date: December 2006
Guests: 200
Topic: An insight in the making of flower rain

"We immediately asked Wiliam where the next flower rain
was held, went there and it was one of the most beautiful
experiences we have ever had!"

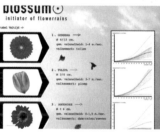

blossum⊙
initiator of flowerrains

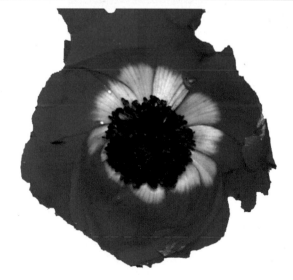

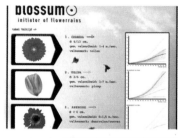

"IF THIS SPILLS INTO THE BUSINESS WORLD, GLOBAL PRODUCTIVITY WILL SKYROCKET AS DEATH-BY-POWERPOINT MEETINGS ARE CUT SHORT. I BELIEVE THE DESIGNERS OF PECHA KUCHA SHOULD BE AWARDED THE NOBEL PRIZE IN ECONOMICS."

RICHARD NANTEL, CEO BRANDON HALL RESEARCH

AN ANTHROPOLOGIST

Presenter: Jan Chipcase
City: Tokyo Vol 35
Date: 9 August 2006
Guests: 450
Topic: Mobile phone repair cultures

修理の生態系
repair eco-system

必要数量のコンポーネント サプライヤ, 卸売業者, 顧客, 知識

critical mass of component suppliers, wholesalers, customers, knowledge

ケータイを修理するという文化
Mobile Phone Repair Cultures
Jan Chipchase

2 0 億 (2 billion)

6 5 億 (6.5 billion)

ホーチミン、デリー、ウランバートル、ソウェト、カンパラ、成都、吉林、厦門、ラサでのリサーチ

research in Ho Chi Minh City, Delhi, Ulan Bataar, Soweto, Kampala, Ji Lin, Chengdu, Xiamen, Lhasa

覆面調査
突撃インタビュー
観察

mystery shopper,
ad-hoc interviews
observations

ソフトウェア & コンテンツ
software & content

保証書
warrantees

平らな面 + スクリュードライバ + ハブラシ + 知識
a flat surface + screwdriver + toothbrush + knowledge

何が目新しいのか？

what's novel?

スケール、コスト、サイズ、他の電子機器と比べた
修理するオブジェクトの普遍性

輸入、半合法的なグレーマーケット、盗難（？）品

優先度と修理にかかる時間

テレビ vs 電話 / エンタメ vs コミュニケーション

scale, cost, size, ubiquity of objects of repair compared to other electronics
imported, grey market, stolen devices (?)
priority & speed of what is repaired
television vs. phone / entertainment vs communication

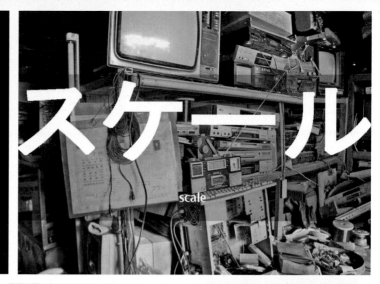

スケール

scale

研修所

aining institutes

THE1ST Photograph for repairing

マニュアル +
manuals +

修理 >> 革新

repair >> innovation

20億 (2 billion)

6 5億 (6.5 billion)

消費者への影響
mplications for consumers

安さ、利便性、速さ、所有コストの軽
減、プロダクトの寿命をより長く

cheap, convenient, fast
reduced cost of ownership
extend lifetime of products

企業への影響
implications for companies

インフォーマルな修理文化から何が学べる
のか？
誰にどんなリスクが？

what can we learn from informal repair
cultures?
what are the risks? for whom?

www.janchipchase.com/repaircultures もどうぞ

"BESIDES LISTENING TO THE PRESENTERS DURING PECHA KUCHA, I LOVE HEARING ABOUT ALL THE POSITIVE THINGS AND COLLABORATIONS HAPPENING AS A DIRECT RESULT OF A PECHA KUCHA NIGHT. AND IN GOTHENBURG THERE ARE MANY EXAMPLES OF THAT!

ARTY RECORD LABEL KNING DISK AND MUSICIAN HIRD PRESENTED AT THE SAME NIGHT AS THE RÖHSSKA DESIGN MUSEUM AND AS A RESULT COPIES OF EACH OF THE KNING DISK RELEASES WERE BOUGHT FOR THE PERMANENT COLLECTION OF THE MUSEUM. ON TOP OF THAT HIRD GOT A JOB ARRANGING CHILL OUT BRUNCH PARTIES EACH SUNDAY AT THE MUSEUM.

THOSE THINGS MAKE ALL THE WORK WORTHWHILE, AND MAKE GOTHENBURG A BETTER CITY."

PKN GOTHENBURG – JESPER LARSSON

A DIRECTOR

Presenter: Peter Cachola Schmal
City: Frankfurt Vol 3
Date: 14 June 2007
Guests: 200
Topic: Police Custody Frankfurt

"Peter is the organizer of Pecha Kucha Frankfurt.
His slides about a closed down German prison
were part of an exhibition, but were also about
the venue of this Pecha Kucha which happened
right there - behind bars! His favorite slide is the
one that reads "Arschlöcher in Grün". It means
"assholes in green" and refers to German police
officers in green uniforms. No one laughed."

Designer Kriengkrit Durongpisitkul talks about his duties in the name of Thai superhero "Kavinman" at Pecha Kucha Bangkok Vol.3

A DANCE COMPANY

Presenter: Strange Kinoko
City: Tokyo Vol 43
Date: 27 June 2007
Guests: 360
Topic: Dance. Performance. Stage. Fun.

珍しいキノコ舞踊団

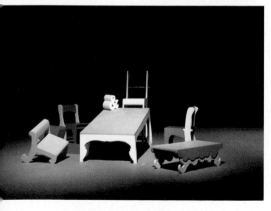

珍しいキノコ舞踊団

あなたの寝顔を
　　　なでてみる。

7月10日〜16日　　吉祥寺シアター
7月22日　　　　　つくばカピオホール
8月15日〜16日　　福岡・IMZホール

TURNING THE INSIDE OUT

When I first came to New York to continue my work for SANAA, I was really disappointed about the architecture scene and I am actually still quite disappointed...

What I really like about Tokyo is the way popular culture is influenced by architecture and the other way around. Casa Brutus magazine does features like "Rem Koolhaas's versus Tadao Ando's fashion". There is just much more ease. In the U.S., architecture is so academic and elite that it doesn't really appeal to a greater audience. There is no general sophistication with architecture and I really miss that about Tokyo.

You have really established architects here in New York: Richard Meier, Steven Holl, etc. But there is actually quite a young evolving scene, too, which is exciting though not so well known. When we organized our first Pecha Kucha about a year ago, it was a real success and brought 500 people. I feel that Pecha Kucha has become the younger generation of architects' event to meet and hang out, but it has also opened up a whole new mixed creative scene.

We didn't want Pecha Kucha to be linked to or associated with one of the established institutes that support the highly sophisticated and elite image of architecture. Rather, in introducing this new format, we wanted to expose architects to a different, unexplored part of the town.

The first Pecha Kucha was in a beer garden in Queens. Then we had one in the Bushwick neighborhood in Brooklyn, but finding a place in Manhattan is really difficult. Now there are certain people who see what is happening and want to be part of it. The Guggenheim Museum, the Museum for Art and Design, and the New Museum are all interested in hosting the next Pecha Kucha. Its funny that we started out avoiding those institutes and now they are coming to us.

Still, we have to find an easier way to get the location and the infrastructure sorted out so that we can focus more on the presentations and the night itself. Especially as I am doing Pecha Kucha on the side while trying to build a museum at the same time!

Organizing events is also something that helps me to show a little bit of me as a person - separate from building another museum. I am about to set up my own architectural practice in New York so extending and reinforcing my network through Pecha Kucha helps me a lot with that.

In terms of selecting our presenters, we try to avoid simple product placements. There are a lot of designers who only want to promote a new chair they built. Instead, we are trying to have a bit more of a message.

We had a guy from Human Rights Watch who has published a report about the construction industry in Abu Dhabi. Since a lot of the architects here are building these big skyscrapers in the Middle East it was really intense for many in the audience to see pictures of the working conditions of those actually constructing their buildings. It made everybody a little quiet for a moment.

People react really differently to the format. You can be a brilliant designer but a terrible speaker, and vice versa. The great thing is the freshness of the format in relation to the overly serious manner in which the design world is usually taken. People tend to add as much weight as possible to what they do, but what's great about Pecha Kucha is its lightness and accessibility. That's why people react so positively to it.

Mark Dytham asked Gregg Pasquarelli from ShoP Architects to present only one day before the event. Gregg just showed up and did it. That means that on the one hand, people can do it well without any preparation, but on the other hand, it is a very difficult format not to prepare for. Strangely contradictory. We have also had some great highly practiced presentations, so all that really counts is to go out there, do it your way and enjoy the opportunity.

Architects in the U.S. are extremely computer savvy, media savvy, and blog oriented. Most of their designs are computer generated and there is a big interest in algorithmics. These architects are very strong behind their machines.

Then, when you actually experience people at a Pecha Kucha Night, it is interesting to see how much of that still holds when those people go out in front of an audience. Architects and especially architecture students live in a very inward-looking isolated world. Pecha Kucha brings them out again and I think that works really well.

Florian Idenburg, PKN New York

AN ARTIST

Presenter: Simon Fernandez
City: Berlin Vol 5
Date: 2 March 2007
Guests: 300 - 350
Topic: His collection of the same Nana Mouskouri
album covers from assorted countries

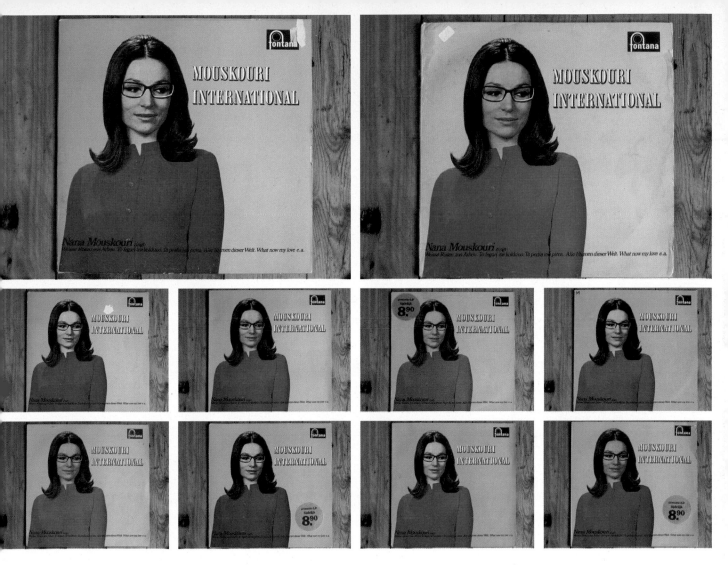

Tom Dixon playing a highly out of tune Kylie Minogue song for some very long 6 minutes and 40 seconds, Pecha Kucha Sydney Vol. 6

SURPRISE PRESENTATION TOPICS

Johnny Vegas (comedian) London
About his old VW Passat

Bruno Maag (font designer) Glasgow
Why Helvetica should be banned!

Cynthia Leung and Beverly Liang (Dear Reader
magazine) New York
About their mothers fashion sense

Joanna Lumley (actress) London
About being a model in the 70s

Jaya Bhatacharji (publisher) New Delhi
History of women's rights poster art in India

Georg Betz (architect) Berlin
Visualization of leg extensions

Takeshi Ishiguro (product designer and inventor)
Tokyo
Presenting a giant smoke ring machine

Temyos Bandhittham (professor) Bangkok
*"Rope access" experience (about climbing high-rise
buildings around the world)*

Jon Snow (news caster) London
Why noone should ever bomb Iran

Kevin Wang (16 years old student) Shanghai
*Achievements of his Photoshop class at Shanghai
International School*

Big Dog (men's underwear designers) Melbourne
Took their clothes off...which was pretty scary!

Jetse Goris (E-learning consultant) Groningen
How to make the biggest water-bomb

Nipa Doshi (designer) London
A vision on life in India

Camelia Wilkinson (Dazzle ships expert) London
About the art of camouflage

Nader Voussoughian (architect, Ph. D. candidate)
New York
*His 3.5 year long doctoral dissertation in 6 minutes 40
seconds to an awe-struck audience.*

Kate Porter (engineer) Sydney
A rundown on the workings of carbon trading markets

Gabi Schirrmacher and Claus Richter (architects)
Frankfurt
*Live baking of famous buildings: Torre Agbar tower
model. Yummy!*

Hou Liang (architect) New York
*How sucking on a fried chicken bone gives him
inspiration for design*

Teddy Otsuka (human rights advocate) Tokyo
Sex, sex, sex!

WELCOME TO
THE WORLD'S
BIGGEST
Pecha Kucha Night

PROGRAMME
DOORS OPEN --
LONDON SCHOOL OF SAMBA ----------------------------- 6.30PM
START --- PLAYING IN THE FOYER
                                                                      7.30PM
MARK DYTHAM + ASTRID KLEIN KLEIN DYTHAM ARCHITECTURE
NIGEL COATES BRANSON COATES
EKOW ESHUN INSTITUTE OF CONTEMPORARY ARTS
AMANDA LEVETE FUTURE SYSTEMS
SEBASTIEN NOEL + CONNY FREYER + EVA RUCKI TROIKA
LIZA FIOR MUF
BERNHARD STEINERHOFF DESIGN CONTROL
INTERVAL --- 8.30PM
RESTARTS --- 9.00PM
SAM JACOB FAT
CHRISTOS PASSAS ZAHA HADID ARCHITECTS
ALISON JACKSON ALISON JACKSON
TOM DIXON TOM DIXON
PAYAM SHARIFI SLAVS
DOMINIC PAPA S333
THOMAS HEATHERWICK HEATHERWICK STUDIO ------ 10.00PM
END ---

BENTLEY   vitra.
BOMBAY SAPPHIRE

THE SPEAKERS

WHY PECHA KUCHA NEEDS A FOUNDATION

One reason why Pecha Kucha has spread virally is because we give it to people for free. It's a bit like some Web 2.0 ventures - a network that is not built on a business plan in the beginning that later turned out to be fruitful.

Luckily this is a ripe time to think about where to go from here.

So far what we have shared at Pecha Kucha are ideas, thoughts multiplied and distributed over many minds. We now want to take Pecha Kucha to the next level. We are setting up a new website to make the Pecha Kucha network more accessible for past presenters and other organizers to get connected and make use of this amazing global database. This way the Pecha Kucha community can grow, connect, and nurture talent around the globe.

Currently we are setting up a Pecha Kucha foundation to give this phenomena of global live events a supporting structure and to make it more accessible to everyone. The goal of the foundation is to work with the Pecha Kucha Network and sponsors to physically realize important, prosocial projects worldwide where they are most needed.

01. Philip Obayda

02. Tsutomu ben sato - bensato arch

03. Takeshi Ishiguro - creative lab

04. Kenzi Murabayashi

05. Kiyoshi Takizawa

06. Ryusuke Nanki & Shun Ikeda

07. Przemek Sobocki

08. Mike Kubeck - SuperDeluxe

SO, HOW DO I SET ONE UP?
Get infected!

- Make sure you are energetic, outgoing, plugged into a creative network and equipped with a proper day-job.

- Remember that Pecha Kucha is an NPO (Non Profit Organization), so make sure you commit yourself to it for the love of sharing ideas and being passionate.

- Write an email to pechakucha@klein-dytham.com telling us a little about your experience, ideas about venues, potential presenters you would like to approach, and your vision for Pecha Kucha in your city.

- Allow some review time.

- Once we think you are the best in your city, we will send you the logos, presentation templates, formats and our infamous "Handshake Agreement" to get you started.

- Commit to holding a Pecha Kucha Night at least four times a year.

- Follow the 20x20 format.

- We will add you to our global website.

- Stay connected with the Pecha Kucha network! Pecha Kucha is about trust and a global awareness. You just read this book. You know what we stand for, so stick with it!

- Welcome to the family!

TONIGHT

PECHAKUCHA
NIGHT
VOL.46

ペチャクチャ ナイト Vol.46

20 x 20 ペチャクチャナイト @ スーパーデラックス

20 枚 x 20 秒

20：20 開始

PRESENTED BY KLEIN DYTHAM ARCHITECTURE
OCTOBER 15TH MONDAY 1000 YEN (1 DRINK IN)

SuperDeluxe

!!!!!!!!!!

GOOD FOOD
MICROBREWED BEER
INTERESTING PEOPLE QUITE OFTEN
AVANT GARDE WOMENS TOILET

THIRSTY?

オリジナル地ビール 700円から
ベルギー産特選瓶ビール 2500円から(750ml)
ワイン＆カクテル 700円から

HUNGRY?

キーマーカレー 900円
ベジタブルカレー 800円
ベジタリアンキリライス 900円
フィッシュアンドチップス 800円
オリジナルスナックス 500円から
スイーツ 400円から

SuperDeluxe

THE TECH SPECS
Here is all you need!

THE EVENT SPACE
- a big room, a garage, a roof - whatever it takes to gather comfortably
- preferably random and flexible seating
- a bar with cool drinks close to the audience
- one or more walls or screens for projections
- one or more bright projectors
- an energetic MC
- microphones (preferably two: for the presenter and the MC)
- a computer containing all the presentations, with connecting cables
- someone taking care of music during the beer break
- a tech-savvy person to stick around for worst case scenarios

THE PRESENTATIONS
- 20 images each from (ideally) 14 presenters, each image being 1024 x 768 pixel jpegs
- visually appealing creative contents only
- no long winded manifestos
- no straight advertising
- no pie charts
- everything swooshed into Apple Keynote (you know, the software that never crashes) and set to 20 seconds per image
- one introductory slide prior to each presentation with the presenter's name projected and a short intro from the MC
- a 20 minute beer break in the middle of the presentations to take a deep breath and a big gulp

Organizers should email the presenters before the event to let them know when they will be on. During the presentation, the presenter has no control over the slides.

An immense round of thanks to the global organizers of Pecha Kucha Night – **Amsterdam:** Bart Cardinaal, Nadine Roos, Joop de Boer, Jeroen Beekmans **Auckland** Luka Hinse, Andrew Barrie, Tim Coster, Robin Martin **Austin, Texas:** Herman Dyal, Carla Fraser **Bangalore:** Naresh V Narasimhan, Dr. Aditya Dev Sood, Rukshana Tavadia, Mrs.Muskaan **Bangkok:** Bioscope Plus, Try2benice Suparp Rimthepathip, Thida Plitpholkarnpim, Surat Tomornsak, Valaikorn Samathakorn **Beijing:** Chen G.Salome, Deller Hanna Miriam, Linack Sebastian, Pucher Florian, Schmidt André, **Belfast:** Rita McCaughey **Berlin:** Iepe Rubingh, Joachim Stein, Luka Hinse, Nadine Freischlad **Bern:** Nora Grunder, Ulrike Habermalz, Peter Bölsterli, Patrick Linder, Irene Krause **Bogota:** Nobara Hayakawa, Alejandro Zamudio **Brisbane:** Kirstie Galloway, Luke Pendergast, Christina Na-Heon Cho **Budapest:** Bujdosó Attila, Finta Sándor, Kertész Monika, Csaba Tímea, Vukoszávlyev Zorán, Tóth Máté **Buenos Aires:** May Groppo, Daniel Abadi, Andy Ovsejevich, Dolores Güemes, GFerna, Blue Vertigo, Mariano Dibiase, Mandetta, Manuchis **Buffalo:** Nick Bruscia, Pete McCarthy, Heamchand Subryan, Mike Baumann, Craig Reynolds, Richard Kegler, Edmund Cardoni, Carolyn Tennant, **Chicago:** Peter Exley, Sharon Exley, Thorsten Bösch, Emma Exley, Jon Langford, Bruce Krippner, Ray Quinn, **Cologne:** Annette Pfeffer, Susanne Junglas **Columbus:** Lindsay Kenzig, Eric Thompson, Jennifer Hehemann, Judy Fratantonio, Robert Patricy, Scott Vayo, Stephanie Patton **Copenhagen:** Morten Engel **Edinburg:** Lynsey Smith, Creative Entrepreneurs Club **Frankfurt:** Peter Cachola Schmal, Arne Winkelmann, Ursula Kleefisch-Jobst, Melanie Schmitt, Börries & Jesper Götsch **Glasgow:** Lynsey Smith, Stacey Hunter, Creative Entrepreneurs Club **Gothenburg:** Jesper Larsson, ADA, Svensk Form Väst, Club Nefertiti **Gröningen:** Mark Hoekstra, Gabriel de Graauw, Rutger Middendorp, Simon Groen, Ambizzious **Hamburg:** Frederik Herr **Helsinki:** Kari Korkman **Hobart:** Aaron Roberts, James Wilson, Nathan Crump **Kuala Lumpur:** Sunitha Janamohanan, Patriana Patrick, Lianna Leong, JUICE mag, Droo, Xu **Las Vegas:** Paul Jamtgaard, Maurice Conti **Los Angeles:** John Southern, Robert Sumrell, Rick Miller **Linz:** Christoph Weidinger, Magnus Hofmüller **Lisbon:** António Pedro Louro, Gonçalo Prudêncio, Pedro Ferreira, Pedro Melo, Rita Joao **Ljubljana:** Maja Vardjan, Matija Bevk, Vasa Perovi, Bla Hartman **London:** Marcus Fairs, Max Fraser, Iram Quraishi **Madrid:** Paloma Hernaiz, Jaime Oliver **Manchester:** Dick Powell **Marseille:** Sarah Carriere-Chardon, Ln Boul, Loic Gestin **Melbourne:** Elida De Felice, Kylie Fitt, Jane Caught, Timothy Moore **Mexico City:** Ania Calderon, Jorge Munguia , Alejandro Ramos, Clorinda Romo, Guillermo Ruiz de Teresa, Sebastian Cárdenas, Arabella Lopezlena **Miami:** Abby Kellett, Max Fraser **Montreal:** Boris Anthony, James Everett **Nagano:** Hitoshi Toyoshima, **Newcastle:** Danielle Pender, Karen Stone, Beckie Darlington **New Delhi:** Dr. Aditya Dev Sood, Shivani Chaitanya Modi, Alice Cicolini, Mike Welch **New York:** Florian Idenburg, Casey Mack, Jon Santos, Seth Adams, Jing Liu, Beverly Liang, Marc McQuade, James Way, Roger Amuruz **Oslo:** Arpna Gupta, Sondre Sommerfelt, Paul Amble, Jørn O. Jøntvedt, Janicke Sæther, Tomas Stokke **Perth:** Natalie Hill, Renae Tapley **Porto Allegre:** Cardoso, Paulo Scott, Lenara Verle, Marcelo Noah, Marcelo Träsel, Fábio Zimbres, A Lavanderia Psicodélica de Charlie Chan, Carla Barth **Prague:** Jana Kostelecká **Riga:** Manten Devriendt, Liene Jakobsone **Rotterdam:** Bart Cardinaal, Nadine Roos, Alex de Jong, Bregje van Woensel, Camera Japan, Inge Jansen, Frija Klijn, Shirin Mirachor **San Francisco:** Paul Jamtgaard, Alberto Villarreal, Dan Senatore, Yuko Naumann **San Jose, Costa Rica:** Mauricio Herrera-Palma, Lindsay Whipp, Andres Cañas **Schiedam:** Bart Cardinaal, Nadine Roos , Caroline Nieuwendijk, Lobke Broos **Seattle:** Ana Pinto da Silva, Paul Jamtgaard **Seoul:** Tesoc, Sungtae Park, Bomi Lee, Yeonsook Choi **Seville:** Pablo Sendra Fernández, Francisco Javier Martínez Navarro, Francisco Castillo Navarro, Fernando Claro Guerrero, José Sánchez-Laulhé Sánchez de Cos, Eva Cristina Jiménez del Río, Patricia Pérez Lucas, Francisco Javier Fernández Gallardo, Elena Morón Ruiz **Shanghai:** Viktor Oldiges, Giel Groothuis, Jinni Lu, Susanne Lorentz, Alan Grillo, Sabrina Qin, Ma Liang, Tim Crowther, Neshat Compani **Stockholm:** Ewa Kumlin, Kajsa Hernell **Stuttgart:** You Seok Na, Mathias Dietsche, Michael Ertel, Hannes Schwertfeger **Sydney:** Marcus Trimble, Steve Toia, Alexandra Matyear, Nicole Bearman, Antoinette Trimble, Joe Snell, Adam Haddow, Jacqui Connor, Eva-Marie Prineas **Taipei:** Fred Chen, Anni Lu, Grace Chen, Jane Cheng, Vacuna Liu **Tel Aviv:** Anat Safran **Tokyo:** SuperDeluxe staff, Mike Kubeck, Namaiki, Chika Muto, Chinatsu Kaneko, Jenny Brown, Atsuko Miyawaki, Tomoko Kagawa, and the KDa Allstars **Toronto:** Jennifer Flores, Sean Stanwick, Samantha Sanella, Gillian Hoff, Jane French, Catherine Molnar, Elyse Parker, Meghan Brousseau, Aleksandra Tasic, **Trieste:** Anna Termite, Mirko Van Den Winkel, Vanna Coslovich, Denis Andrian, Sara Barnaba, Lisa Corva, Manuel Costantin, Giovanni Damiani, Roberta Debernardi, Thomas Bisiani, Federico Gori **Udine:** Anna Termite, Mirko van den Winkel, Thomas Bertacche, Massimo Burello, Emiliano Calderoni, Cristina Casarsa, Paolo Jacob, Marco Villotta, Tania Mlinar, Gianluca Uliana, Gianni De Luise, Lucrezia Armano, Luca Piazza, Sandro, Brunno Jahara, Maurizio Galluzzo, Vanna Coslovich, Denis Andrian, Sara Barnaba, Lisa Corva, Manuel Costantin, Giovanni Damiani, Roberta Debernardi, Thomas Bisiani, Federico Gori, Kristal Blanco, Werner Chert, Tommaso Michieli, Furio Barzon, Adriana Cruciatti, Renata Ballarin **Venice:** Anna Termite, Mirko van den Winkel, Lucrezia Armano, Luca Piazza, Sandro, Brunno Jahara, Maurizio Galluzzo **Vienna:** Max Kamenar, Franz Sumnitsch **Wellington, New Zealand:** Luka Hinse

Our deepest gratitude to all of the Pecha Kucha Night presenters— 366, 791, (N55), oooyo, 2aMO, 3JV, 45treinta, 4ta Pared, 6.40 Degraus, a.s*, Aad Krol, Aamu Song, Ab Rogers, Abby Hewitson, Abhishek Hazra, Acampante, Achim Menges, Ácido Surtido, Ada Tolla, Adam Brouillette, Adam Gebrian, Adam Haddow, Adam Jenns, Adam Khamis, Adam Oostenbrink, Adam Rouse, Adam Scott, Adele Varcoe, Aditya Pande, Adnan Harambasic, Adriana Berrío, Adriana Lindquist, Aeron Bergman, Afaina de Jong, Aforest Design, Afshin Mehin, Aga and Sun, Agustin Peña, Ai Kurahashi, Aiko, Aino, Brandt, AJ Kandy, Akemi Tazaki, Akihito Fumita, Akiko Asaco, Akiko Miyaguch, Akira Hikone, Akira Wakita, Akshai Sarin, Al Nader Vossoughian, Alain Bruner, Alain Fidanza, Alan Burden, Alan Záruba, Alastair Adair, Alastair Forbes, Alastair Fuad-Luke, Albano Garcia, Albert Kramer, Albert lee, Albert Tang, Alberto Licandro, Alberto Villarreal, Aldo Chaparro, Alejandra Salinas, Alejandro Hernández, Alejandro M Lopez, Alejandro Martín, Alejandro mayo, Alejandro Zamudio, Ales Najbrt, Alessandro Lepore, Alessandro Munge, Alessia De Palma, Alessio Princic, Alex Barker, Alex Berman, Alex Craig, Alex Cruikshank, Alex de Jong, Alex de Rijike, Alex Dorfsman, Alex Jaimes, Alex Karr, Alex Nieminen, Alex Pettas, Alex Ramos, Alex Rich, Alex Roberts, Alexander Lervik, Alexander Ljung, Alexander Lotersztain, Alexander Peli, Alexander Radoske, Alexander Schärer, Alexander Taylor, Alexandra Deschamps-Sonsino, Alexandra Loew, Alexandra Suhner, Alexandra Verhaest, Alexandre Armond, Alexia Somerville, Alfredo Genovese, Algorritmo, Alice Babidge, Alice Fung, Alice Jagtman, Alice Schock, Alice Wang, Alicia Rosam, Alicia Velazquez, Alison Jackson, Alison Jambert, Alistair Sim, Aljosa Bagola, Aljosa Dekleva, Allard van Hoorn, Allegra McCoy, Almira Sadar, Álmosdi Árpád, Alvaro Verduzco, Amale Andraos, Amanda Levete, Amanda Parkes, Amandeep Jawa, Amandititita, Amelia Noble, Ames Asbell, Amina Abdala, Amit Berlowitz, Ammon Rost, Amos Klausner, Ana Belen Paizanni, Ana Dzokoc, Ana Pinto da Silva, Ana Ramos, Anab Jain, Ananth Sampathkumar, Anat Safran, Anders Arentoft, Anders Hofgaard, Anders Nereim, André Heinz, André Nossek, Andrea B. Hetzel, Andrea Destefanis, Andrea Djerf, Andrea Green Kobayashi, Andrea Hikone, Andrea Larsen, Andrea Lenardin-Madden, Andrea Ling, Andreas Arnildm, Andreas Gärtner, Andreas Gebhard, Andreas Lyckefors, Andreas Meichsner, Andreas Meichsner, Andreas Moser, Andreas Nobel, Andres Cañas, Andrés de Santiago Areizaga, Andres Holguin, Andrés Romero Baltodano, Andrew Barrie, Andrew Burns, Andrew Chetty, Andrew Frost, Andrew Hamilton, Andrew Harding, Andrew Klemmer, Andrew Lantz, Andrew MacNair, Andrew Missingham, Andrew Pingle, Andrew R. Chambers Jr, Andrew Sheppard, Andrew Silke, Andrew Weldon, Andy Davey, Andy Hall, Andy Lee, Andy MacDonald, Andy Marks, Andy Stevens, Andy T, Anet Kuhla, Angela Dytham, Angela Oakes, Angelica Burtscher, Angelo Betti, Angie Waller, Ania Dabrowska, Anila Rubiku, Anja Koch, Ann Yamamoto, Anna Hesse, Anna Lund, Anna Schori, Anna Sjons Nilsson, Annabel Dundas, Annaeline, Annapuna Garimela, Anne Brodie, Anne Nelsen, Anne Warr, Anne-Sophie Heist, Annette Etges, Annie Han & Daniel, Ansgar Oberholz, Anthony Bello, Antje Krause-Wahl, Antoine Boilevin, Antoine Català, Anton Savov, Antonio García Madrigal, Antônio Xerxenesky, Antonio Yemail, AntsTokyo, Binta Bon, Antti Hinkula, Aprily Zoltán, Arata Naya, Arcangel Constantini, Archana Prasad, Archi TV, Architecture Students from Temple University, Architekturkommando, Ard Boer, Arend-Jan Majoor, Ariadna Cantis, Ariel Orozco, Ariel Schlesinger, Ariel Winograd, Arijana Gadzijev, Arjo Rozendaal, ARM, Arne Quinze, Arne Winkelmann, Arno Coenen, Arno Schmitz, Arnoud Schuurman, Arnout Van Mameren, Arq Clorindo Testa, Arq Jujo Solsona, Arq.Rafael Ayala Balboa from taller 13 Arquitectos, Arquitectos Pretterhofer Spath, Arsene Bardis, Art Zendarski, Artmongers, Artur Moustafa, Asao Tokolo, Åshild Sævik, Asif Khan, Astrid Klein, atı03, Ateliermob, Atmosfera, Atsuhiro Ito, Atsuko Miyawaki, Atul Bhalla, Augusto Costhanzo, Auli Laitinen, Aurelie Nangniot, Aurora Jovan, Aurora Mahassine, Auston Lee, Axel StockBurger, Ayako Maruta, Ayumi Han, Azby Brown, Aziza Chouni, Backa Karin Ivarsdotter, Bagi Tamas, Balz Mueller, Bang Phan, Barbara Bestor, Barbara Della Polla, Barbara Uderzo, Barbora Klímová, Barcza Gergely, Barend Koolhaas, Barnaby Barford, Barnaby Bennett, Barry Threw, Bart Cardinaal, Bart Haney, Bart Overly, Bart van Lieshout, Bas Princen, Bas Van Raay, Bea Seggering, Beardyman, Beatrice Leanza, Bee Futon, Behzad Farazollahi, Ben Aranda, Ben Gabel, Ben List, Ben McCarthy, Ben O'Brien, Ben Oostrum, Ben Parco, Ben Wilkie, Benedek Botond, Beni Reusser, Beniamino Saibene, Benjamin Graindorge, Benjamin Lin, Benny Adrion, Berhard Strecker, Bernard Whitcher, Bernhard Franken, Bernhard Steinerhoff, Bert de Munck, Bert Hadders, Bert Hümmels, Berti Distelrath, Berto Pandolfo, Beth Blostein, Beth Lieberman, Betty Wimmer, Beverly Liang, Biba Meira, Bibi Cordix Lowe, Bill Mckay, Bill Yen, Biyaan Tomohiko Amemiya, Bjoern Melhus, Björn Dahlström, Bjorn Wijers, Bjørnar Johnsen, Blank, Bleed, Bo Yee Poon, Bob Sanderson, Bobby Baker, Böczén Árpád, Bodo Sperlein, Bodo Sperlein, Bokudes, Bollinger+Grohmann ingenieure, Bond Lieu, Börries & Jesper Gotsch, Boubi Luxembourg, Bozzolla Gallardo, Brad Pinchuk, Bram Dauw, Bram Esser, Brandon Shigeta, Brandon Warren, Brendan Cowell, Brendan Dawes, Brendan McGetrick, Brent Stringfellow, Brett Leonhardt, Brett Stilwell, Brian Donohue, Brian Grunert , Brian Hartley, Brian Harvey, Brian Rasmussen, Brian Silverman, Briar Shaw, Britt Salt, Bronwyn Streader, Brook Andrew, Brook Banham, bru and cherioe architects, Bruce Beasley, Bruce Kuwabara, Brunno Jahara, Bruno 9li, Bruno Giuntoli, Bruno Maag, Bryan Calo, Bryce Gibson, BsAs Sonora, Bubu, Bujdosa Attila, Burak Pekoglu, Burton Baldridge, Byul, C David Tseng, C. J. Lu, Callie Roach, Calvin Chen, Camalo Gaskin, Cameron Robbins, Camiel Voorn, Camila Mazzini, Camilla Wilkinson, Camila Garcia, Camilo Hernandez, Camilo Peláez, Can2, Caramel, Cardoso, Carl Burdick, Carl Douglas, Carla Barth, Carlo Nordloh, Carlos Bunga, Carlos Trilnik, Carol Bensimon, Carole Lévesque, Carolien Vleiger, Carolina Blue, Carolina Melis, Carolina Rey, Caroline Blais, Caroline Ogez, Caroline Robbie, Carolyn Tennant, Casey Mack, Caterina Ongaro, Catriona Paterson, Céline Fiammante, Céline Papion, Cesar Mena Rivero, CesarCedano, Chalermchatri Yukol, Chalita Chamnianwai, Champignon, Chan Wei-hsiung, Chantalle McDonald, Charles Baker, Charles Merewether, Charles Renfro, Charley Bauer, Charlie Koolhaas, Charlie Sheldon, Charlie Xia, Charlotte Schroner, Chas Pope, Chasey Mack, Chatchaval Khonkajee, Chaves, Chiba, Chie Nabeshima, Chieko Miyagawa, Chihiro Morita, Chi-ho Kim, Chihoko Miyagama, Chika Muto, Chinatsu Kaneko, Chisa Toda, Chizuko Takinami, Chonlathon Pothong,

...ris Bowman, Chris De Campo, Chris Kirby, Chris Lasch, Chris Lee, Chris Luomanen, Chris Major, Chris Money Piatt, Chris Ottley, Chris Osborne, Chris
Palmieri, Chris Pommer, Chris Ritke, Chris Romano, Chris Sanderson, Chris Silverthorn, Christey Johansson, Christiaan Cruz, Christian Janecke, Christian
Jankowski, Christian Kaestner, Christian Lemon, Christian Noll, Christian Schneider, Christian Simons, Christian Skovgaard, Christian Waldvogel, Christian
Whopperer, Christian Wiedersheim, Christian Wopperer, Christian Zanatta, Christina E. Dechau, Christina Cho, Christina Clark, Christina Martin, Christina
Ulke, Christina Waterson, Christina Zeidler, Christine Istad, Christine Istad, Christine Kwong, Christine Pilsl, Christine Tarkowski, Christoffer Berg, Christoph
Cellarius, Christoph Helzle, Christoph Moeskes, Christoph Peterka, Christoph Schenk, Christoph Stark, Christophe Bailleux, Christophe Koch, Christophe
Hewson, Christopher Kaltenbach, Christos Marcopoulos, Christos Passas, Chuck Hoberman, Chun Woei, Chuo Yuan-Ping, Chutharut Pornmuneesoonton,
Ciro najle, Clare Robinson, Claudia Battaino, Claudia Reisenberger, Claudius Gagalka, Claus Richter, Claus Staniek, Clemens Weisshaar, Clement Gros, Club
del Disco, Club Real, Co Iwama, CODA, Cody Hudson, Coichi Wada, Colectivo Bricolaje, Colectivo Fierro, Colectivo Metapono, Colin Finnegan, Colin Kahn,
Colin Schaelli, Colonel Blimp, Complizen, Co-nekt, Connie Chen, Corbett Griffith, Corinna Cadetto, Cory Worth, Courtney Grim, Craig Bond, Crear vale la
pena, Crispijn van Sas, Crispin Jones, Cristina Bolis, Cristina Chiappini, Cristina Lei Rodriguez, Csaba Timea, Csanády Pál, ctrlshifto7, Culebrón Timbal,
CultureDrone, Cynthia Leung, Cyril Ríha, D H Rosen, Daan Roosegaarde, Dadara, Daffyd Burne Jones, Dagmar Reinhardt, Dainippon Type Organization,
Daisuke Furusawa, Dale Phurough, Daljit Singh, Damasio, Damian Barr, Damian Fossati, Damn Laser Vampires, Damon Rich, Dan Corson, Dan Fern, Dan
Hodler, Dan Honey, Dan Wood, Dan Ziglam, Dana Bauer, Dana Kreiger, Danidan, Daniel Aisenson, Daniel Cisneros, Daniel Daou, Daniel Eatock, Daniel Erler,
Daniel Glauser, Daniel Josefsohn, Daniel Parker, Daniel Rehn, Daniel Spacek, Daniel Tobias Etzel, Daniel Traub, Daniel Valle, Daniel von Bernstorff, Daniel
Warrington, Daniela Elbahara, Daniele Lupo, Daniele Mattioli, Danielle Freakley, Dany Lyons, Daphne Bom, Dara Huang, Darin Bendall, Dario Colombo,
Dario Romagnoli, Darja Cancíková, Darren Adair, Datenstrudel, Dave Anderson, Dave Praeger, David A. Moore, David Adjaye, David Andreen, David Baker,
David Breil, David Chaloner, David Chaloner, David deHeilly, David Elliott, David Fisher, David Freer, David Henshaw, David Hicks, David Keech, David
Kopecky, David Kraus, David Lancashire, David Levene, David Mastalka, David Presley, David Reinfurt, David W. Dieter, David Welsh, David Wilson, David
Winston , Davide Crippa, Davide Scalenghe, Davina Rooney, Davor Bruketa, Deak Daniel, Dean Manning, Deborah Kang, Deborah Richmond, Deborah Saunt,
Defne Ayas, Demetri Estdelacropolis, Denis Guzzo, Dennis Maher, Dennis Rudolph, Department of Architecture University of California, design zero,
Designkommando, DG PH, Diana Mangaser, Dick el demasiado, Dick Powell, Diederik Corvers, Diederik Corvers, Diego Agudelo-Gallo, Diego Berruecos,
Diego Taborda, Diego Teo, Diego Vargas, Dieguez Fridman, Dienes Vivien, Dieter Strauch, Dimitri Waltritsch, Dinah Casson, Dinne Bosman, Dion Narnia, Dir
Hebel, Dirk Jan Postel, Dirk Zimmerman, Dirkje Bakker, dit is dit, Diwata Tharan, Dixie, Dizajn na Kolesách, DJ. Puri Puri, Do Young Chung, Dolores, Dom
Chotivanich, Doma, Domenico Bartolo, Domenico Redavid, Dominic Dube, Dominic Keating, Dominic Papa, Don Paul Swain, Donald Euban, Roos
Donald Schmitt, Dongfang Gao, Donna Wingate, Doris Sung, Doug Motz, Doug Pritchard, Douglas Dickel, Douglas Hendry, Douglas Ho, Dr oper
Dr. Ivan Poupyrev, Dr. Stefan Lehnert, Dr.Takerng Pattanopas, Dragon, Drazen Dragojevic, Dror Benshetrit, Duncan Griffin, Dusic & ddilddil, Dusita Imarom
Eakasit Thairaat, Ed Barber, Ed Hollis, Ed Marszewski, Ed Robinson, Eddy Kaijser, Ede Bopp, Edgar González, Edouard Vincent, Eduardo Olivares, Eduardo
Torres, Edward Eglin, Edward Suzuki, Edwina Lin, Eero Koivisto, Efe Cakare, Egied Simons, Egle, Einar Aarvig, Eisuke Tachikawa, Ekip, Ekow Eshun, El Jardín,
Elbert Arens, Elena Carlini, Eliel Johnson, Eline van der Laag, Elinor Whidden, Ellen de Vries, Elliot Brooke, Elsa Seefahrt, Elukka Eskelinen, Emiko Miki, Emiko
Oki, Emilia Terragni, Emilio García Wehbi, Emily White, Emitflesti, Emma Booty, Emma Lewis, Emma Telfer, Emma Thomas, Emma-Cecillia, Emmanuel Gilloz,
Emmanuel Guillard, Emmanuel Picault, Engenhart Visuelle, EnREDo, Enric Ruiz, Enrico Taranta, Eric Bunge, Eric Leleu, Eric Marechal, Eric Wahlforss, Erica
Wagner, Erich Martino, Erik Adigard, Erik Escalante, Erik van Loon, Eriko Mikami, Erin Cubbison, Erja Hirvi, Erlend Haffner, Erlend Kyte, Erosie, Erwin Pols
Escuadrón Mutante, Esperanto Foreningen, Esteban de Manuel, Esteban Gutierrez, Ester Kroezenga, Esther Didden, Esther Hong, Esther van der Eerden,
Etienne Reijnders, Eugene Low and Matthew Ng, Eugenio Murillo, Eun-ah Seol, Eunjung Hwang, Eva, Eva Castro , Eva M. Brekkestø, Ewa Kumlin, Ewan
Umrie, Ewan McEoin, Ewen Spencer, F Huesped, Fabian and Lisa, Fabiane Perrella, Fabiano Gummo, Fabio D' Agnano, Fabio Gigone, Fabio Godoh, Fabio
Novembre, Fabrice Koukoui, Faktum, FAT, Federico Díaz, Federico Rodriguez, Federico Soriano, Federico Uribe, Fehér Beatrix, Feiko Beckers, feld72, Felip
Beltrán, Felipe Lopez, Felipe Mesa, Felix Goebel, Felix Madrazo, Felix Nowak, Femke Bijlsma, Fennel Wolcott Doyle, Ferdinand Oswald, Fernanda Chemale
Fernando Brízio, Fernando Callender, Fernando Claro, Fernando Herrera, Fernando Llanos, Fernando Marín, Fernando Mesta, Fernando Pérez, Filete, Filip
Cenek, Final Home, Finta Sándor, Fiona Leus, Fiona Milligan, Fiona Raby, Fish S. Hasegawa, Florencia Braga Menéndez, Florencia Kohan, Florencia Pita
Florian Schreiter, Floris Maathuis, Flúor Design, Fogo na Franja, Folkform, Forster/Chirotarrab, Frag Woodhall, Franca Pauli, Francesca Savoia, Francesco
Gatti, Francisco A. Ortega, Francisco Castillo Navarro, Francisco David Boira, Francisco Fernández Gallardo, Francoise Lamy, Frank Beelen, Frank Havermans
Frank Krueger, Frank La Riviere, Frank Minnaert, Franka Diehnelt, Franl La Riviere, Frans Veenhoven , Franz Ammann, Franz Sumnitsch, Fred Chen, Fred
Hatt, Fred Schurink, Frederic Heidenberg, Frederico Duarte, Frederik, Freek Homan, Freek van Arkel, FREITAG, Frida Fjellman, Friedrich Kirschner, Friedrich
Liechtenstein, Friso Gouwetor, Fukaura Tomoshige, Fuldesign, Fumi Saito, Fumio Inoue, Fundación Ph15, Funk Bogdán, Gabe Ulacco, Gabi Bern an, Gabi
Schirrmacher, Gabriel de Graauw Platform Gras , Gabriela Bejerman, Gareth Williams, Garrett Britton, Gary Cruce, Gaspar Libedinsky, Gautam Mali, Gaylen
Preston, Gazz, Genevieve Blanchett, Geoff Cape, Georg Betz, Georg Riesenhuber, George Iwasawa, Georgie and Alex Cleary, Georgina Huljich, Ger C. Bout
Geraldo Tavares, Gerard O'Conner, Gerardo Hochman, Gerardo Recoder, Gerbes Gábor, Gero Grudmann, Gheorg Mug, Ghuz Dsign, Gideon Obarzanek, Gio

Groothuis, Gilson Vargas, Ginger Wolfe, Giovanni Ozzola, Gira Industria, Giulio Calderini, Giulio Cappellini, Giulio Polita, Giuseppe Lignano, Gladys Jacobson, Glanzkinder, Glenn Lym, Go Hasegawa, G▮▮o Justino, Gonzague Verdenal, Gopika Nath, Gorazd Ma▮▮Gorbet Design Inc, Gordon Murray, Gosia Gruba, Gozi Ochonogor, Grant Gibson, Grant Warmerdam, Grayson Perry, Grayson Stallings, Greenpeace, Greg McNamara, Gregg Pasquarelli, Gregor Podnar, Gregory Larin , Gregory Pierre, Gualtiero Victor Spiro Jaeger, Gudi Schwienbacher, Guido Indij, Guido Stazinski, Guilherme Dable, Gummi Brynjarsson, Gunjan Gupta, Gunter und Umtzi, Gunther Zsolt, Guntis Zingis, Guru Guru sign, Gustaf Ingers, Gustaf Nordenskiold, Gustavo Nielsen, Gutai Mátyás, Guus Vreeburg, Guy Keulemans, Guzmán Yarza, Gwenael Nicolas, Gwendolyn Burkin, Gys Arkitekter, Gyz la Riviere, H3L, Hadi Ghaemi, Haig Djambazian, Hajime Masubuchi, Hamish Neville, Hanan Pomagrin, Hanna Harris, Hanna Petrine Munkeby, Hannah Bonjer, Hanne Rivrud, Hanneke Laaning, Hannes Koch, Hannes Kraft, Hannes Saxer, Hannu Kähönen, Hans Kloeti, Hans Kok, Hans Lerperger, Hans Matthew, Harada Mao, H▮▮a Masahiro, Harmen Liemburg, Harriet McDonald, Harry Woodrow, Hartmut Landauer, Haruaki Tanaka, Haruka Kuryu, Harvest, Hashimoto Yukio, Hatsue Tsunoda, Hatvani Ádám, Hazime Horiuchi, He Yan, Heather Roberge, Hector Castillo, Hector Falcón, Heikki Ruoho, Heiko Michels, Hein van Da▮▮Helen Gill Wright, Helena Baude, Helene Defilippi, Helge Bomber Steinmann, Helka Parkkinen, Hendrikjan Grievink, Henk Aron, Henk Bultstra, ▮▮nk-Jan Willems, Hennie Smit, Henning Basler , Henrik Thodesen, Henrik Valeur, Hernando Barragán, Hester Orlemans, Heta Kuchka, Hideaki Kawa▮▮, Hideki Nakajima, Hidemasa Hirosawa, Hideo Nakayasu, Hikaru Hattori, Hiro Sugiyama, HiroeTanita, Hirohiko Sakane, Hirokawa Junya, Hiroki Matsuura, Hiroki Tanabe, Hiroko Oda, Hiroko Shiratori, Hiroko Takeshima, Hiroko Takeshita, Hiromichi Yasuda, Hironao Tsuboi, Hironori Iwasaki, Hiroshi Ito, Hiroshi Kawano, Hiroshi Kikuchi, Hiroshi Nakamura, Hiroshi Ninomiya, Hiroshi Yoneya, Hirotaka Satoh, Hiroto Aranishi, Hiroto Kubo, Hiroyasu Shoji, Hiroyuki Matsukage, Hisako Sugiura, Hisashi Taniguchi, Hisayama Yukinari, Hitomi Udagawa, Hitoshi Nakanishi, Hitoshi Toyoshima, Hnos Estebecorena, Holger Kehne, Holm Friebe, Hou Liang, Hrvoje Njiric, Huey Ying Hsu, Hugh Snellgrove, Hugo Tillman, Huibert Groenendijk, Hun Kim , Hunter Hendrickson, Huschang Pourian, Huseyin Sami, Huszár András, Hyeon seong Kim, Hyun-jin Baek, I Ragazzi Della Prateria, Ian Lynam, Ian Moore, Ian Rudge, Ian Stallard, Ianus Keller, Idealice, Idee Liu, Iepe Rubingh, Ieve Holthausen, Igor Kovacevic, Igor Medjugorac, IJsbrand van Leeuwen, Ikeda Ryoko, Ilana Mitchel▮▮ja Knezovic, Ilkka Suppanen, Ilse Crawford, Imanaga Kazutoshi, Ine Keitz, Ine Keitz, Ineke Heerkens, Inés Berton, Ingalill Wahlroos-Ritter, Ingerid H Almaas, ingo Niermann, Ingrid Peña Sánchez, Inkahoots, intentionallies, Iole Alessandrini, Ippei Katsumi, Ippei Matsumoto, Irakli Eristavi, Iram Quarishi, Irena Fialová, Irene Tobón, Irupé Tárrago Ros, Isabelle Goris, Isamu Yoda, Isao Hosoe, Ise, Ismar Enriquez, Issara Panchapornphol, Itsuko Hasegawa, Iva Resetar, Iván Chacón, Ivan Galuzin, Ivan Hernández, Ivan Mora, Ivan Palacky, Ivan Shumkov, Ivana Verle, Ivánka Katalin, Ivo Langenick, Izat, Iztok Kovac, Izuldin Hani, Izumi Okayasu, J.T. Rinker, Ja Jun Mao, Jaakko van 't Spijker, Jack Fisher, Jack Mc Kinney, Jackkrit Anantakul, Jacob Mathew, Jacob van Rijs, Jacobo García-Germán, Jacqueline Paglialonga, jae hyouk Sung, Jaime Hayon, Jake Smallman, Jakob Granit, Jakpong Siririn, Jakub Berdych, James Bowskill, James Brearley, James Brucz, James Chang, James Clar, James Gardiner, James Goggin, James Grieshaber, James Grimley, James Hebbert, James Mair, James Medcraft, James Newitt, James Rojas, James Russell, James Tsai, James Warrington, Jamie Mclellan, Jamin, Jan Camp, Jan Chipchase, Jan Coerts, Jan Felix Clostermann, Jan Jongert, Jan Kaláb, Jan Kaplicky, Jan Nemecek, Jan Northoff, Jan Schindler, Jan Tanaka, Jan van de Til, Jan Yoshiyuki Tanaka, Jana Tichá, Jane Pierce, Jani Joenniemi, Janine Reichel, Janjaap Ruijssenaars, Janne Eraker, Janne Kyttanen, Jan-Wessel Hovingh, Jaroslav Róna, Jaroslav Wertig, Jason Chyi, Jason Lee, Jasper Noldus, Jatinder Verma, Javier Belmont, Javier Elguea, Javier Lozano, Javier Ponce, Jay Gopal, Jay Lim and Vivian Toh, Jay Osgerby, Jaya Bhattacharji, Jean Snow, Jean Ulrich Desert, Jean-Benoit Levy, Jeanine Centuori, Jef Biesinger, Jeff Barrett, Jeff Gaines, Jeff Traer, Jefferson Hack, Jeffrey Krause, Jelien Veenstra , Jen Adrion, Jenna Didier, Jenny Holmes, Jens Harder, Jens Thiel, Jens Thoms Ivarsson, Jep▮▮jgård, Jeremy Cheval, Jeremy Hansen, Jeremy Randerson, Jeremy Sutton, Jeroen Beekmans, Jeroen Bisscheroux , Jeroen Everaert, Jeroen Jongeleen, Jeroen Koolhaas, Jerome Kugan, Jerome Pasquero, Jesper Bange, Jesper Larsson, Jesse Nickerson, Jessica Fellowes, Jessica Graham, Jetse Goris, Jettamon Malayota, Jewboy, Ji Ji, Ji-a Chang, Ji-hoon Ha, Jihyuk Park, Jin hee Yoo, Jin Shimoda, Jindrich Stary, Jing Lu, Jinhee Park, Jinko Nakamura, Jiri Cernicky, Jiri David, Jiří Havlícek, Jiro Endo, Jiro Kamata, Jitske Hagens, Jo Jackson, Jo Nagasaka, Jo Shaw, Joachim Baan, Joachim Frost, Joachim Müller-Lancé, Joachim Sauter, Joachim Stein, Joanna Bell, Joanna Lumley, Joanne Jakovich, João Luís Carrilho da Graça, Joe Gebbia, Joe Hiscott, Joe MacDonald, Joe Magliaro, Joe Matthiessen, Joe Moss, Joeke & Marijne Beenhakker, Joel Veitch, Joep Geelen, Johan Bettum, Johan Brouwer, Johan de Wachter, Johan Kleinjan, Johan Olsson, Johan Prag, Johannes Reinsch, John Cary, John Edmark, John Hassay, John Hillier, John Hong, John Lyall, John Nordon, John Pasden, John Radford, John Southern, John Tong, Johnny Vegas, Johnson Chou, Jon Hall, Jon Langford, Jon Løvøen, Jon Santos, Jon Simon, Jon Snow, Jon Yongfook Cockle, Jonas Nordgren, Jonas Ravlo Stokke, Jonas Stokke, Jonas Wagell, Jonathan Atkinson, Jonathan Clarke, Jonathan Webb, Joop de Boer, Joost Haasnoot, Joost Merema, Jopo de Gomina, Jordan & Stenberg, Jörg Schwertfeger, Jörg Stollmann, Jorge Amigo, Jorge Furuya, Jorge Haro, Jorge Restrepo, Jörh Hejkal, Joris Sparenberg, Joris van Hoytema, Jorrit Verduin, José Adrião, José de la Rosa, José Luis Martín, Jose María Cabeza Laínez, José Morales, José Pérez de Lama, Jose va▮▮er Loop, Josefin Lassbo, Joseph Miceli, Josephine Gianni, Josh Kornfeld, Josh Lefers, Josh Usher, Joshua Decter, Josta de Hoog, Josune Garcia-Yangua▮▮Jovan Jelovac, Juan Carlos Tello, Juan David Giraldo, Juan Felipe Rubio, Juan Pablo Corvalán, Judy Fratantonio, Juerg Lehni, Juha Itkonen, Juhana Arkio, Juho Grönholm, Jukka Halminen, Julia Barnes, Julia Deville, Julia Geirtz, Julia Gritzka, Julia Ogrydziak, Julia Wang, Julian Fox, Julian Montague, Julián Reboratti, Julian Roberts, Julian Williams, Julian Worrall, Julie Fjeldstad, Julie Jiang, Julie Murchinson, Julie Schwartz, Julie Stout, Julie Verhoeven, Juliejosiane, Julien Dupont, Jun Aoki, Jun Fujinuma, Jun Hirasawa, Jun Kato, Jun sung Kim, Jun Yanasigawa, Junco Matsuoka, Jung-in Choi, Jun-Hi

Wehrergen, Junichi Hirasawa, Janko Hoshizawa Sedlak, Junpei Kizu, Jumpei Ohno, Junya Ishigami, Junya Masuda, Juraj Horvath, Jürgen Mayer H., Jürgen Müller, Jurij Sadar, Justin Schmidt, Justin Trendall, Justus Slaakweg , Justy Phillips, Jutha Sukawanich, Juthathip Techachumreon, Jyri Engestrom, Kagaj Masaki, Kahori Maki, Kai Bergmann, Kai Otto, Kaije Feenstra, Kait Prystupa, Kajsa Nordstrom, Kalmár László, Kamil Mrva, Kamila Amblerová, Kamiya Setsu Kampanart Heanchasri, Kanako Sekiguchi, Kaname Arauchi, Kaname Arauchi, Kanenobu Baba, Kaori Murata, Kaori Tsuji, Kaoru Mende, Kara Besher, Karen Mauney-Brodek, Karen Toftegård, Karen Walker, Karin Kruse, Karl Dubost, Karl Holmqvist, Karla Brunet, Karmelina Martina, Karmen Franinovic, Karolina Keyzer, Karolina Kling, Kars Alfrink, Kasia Wydroski, Kaspar Koenig, Kasper B. Borg, Katarina Sevic, Katarina Sjögren, Kate Bezar, Kate Orff, Kate Porter Katelyn Fraser, Katerina Vincourová, Katharina Mantel, Katherine Melcher, Kathy Lette, Kati Rubinyi, Katie Hepworth, Katriina Lankinen, Katrin Tersteger Katsuhiko Hibino, Katsuji Konishi, Katsunori Aoki, Katsunori Nishi, Kayoko Asakura, Kazue Monno, Kazuhiko Kawahara, Kazuhiko Namba, Kazuhiro Kojima Kazuhiro Kosugi, Kazuko Hishiya Music, Kazutoshi Imanaga, Kazuyo Sejima, Kedem Shinal, Kei Fukuda, Keiji Ashazawa, Keiko Nakagawa, Keisuk Kobayashi, Keisuke Oda, Keisuke Toyoda, Keith + Lottie, Keith Dodd, Keizaburo Honda, Keizo Maeda, Kelly Malec-Kosak, Kelner Krisztián, Kemény Vagyim Ken Kaizu, Ken Nakanishi, Ken Tarlow, Ken Tsai Lee, Ken Yokogawa, Kenichi Togawa, Kenji nawa, Kenny Tang, Kenta Kishi, Kenya Miura, Kenzi Murabayash Kerati Narkhanark, Kerr Blyth, Kerry Adams Hapner, Kerstin Schultz, Kerstin Sylwan, Kestutis, Kevin Curren, Kevin Finn, Kevin Gibson, Kevin Johansen Khanchit Vanichdilokkul, Khusroo Kalyanwala, Kie Ellens, Kiefer Wang, Kim Engbers, Kim Krech, Kinley Caliper , Kir Royal alias Karin Hofko, Kiran Shiva Aka. Kiran Subbaiah, Kiran Venkatesh, Kirsty Carter, Kiss Gergely, Kiss Ida, Kito, Kitschic, Kittirat thamprajamjit, Kiyomi Kodama, Kiyoshi Takizawa, Kjell Grant Kjell Grant, Kjersti Monson, Klaas Diersmann, Knut Bry, Ko Pinpin, Kobayashi Eriko, Kochi Kazuyasu, Koert van Mensvoort, Koichi Okamoto, Koichi Suzunc Koichiro Shima, Komsun Nuntachit, Konno-kun, Koos de Jong, Kopkit Tangpanthong, Kornkrit Jianpinidnan, Kosuke Fujitaka, Kosuke Idee, Kosuke Shimizu Kou Yoshitaka, Kouji Uchiyama, Kovács Bence, Kovács Gergely, Kozue Nakamura, Krajcsi Sarolta, Krause, Kriengkrit Durongpisetkul, Kris Holmes, Kri: Knook, Krisann Rehbein, Krista Blake, Kristal Blanco, Kristian Skylstad, Kristina Schipper, Kristina Svensson, Kristof Kintera, Kristoffer, Kubota Shigeru Kugler Péter, Kumi Aizawa, Kunal Ghevaria, Kunal Ghevaria & Chloe, Kung Shu-Chang, Kuniko Meada, Kunle Adeyemi, Kuro-chan, Kyle Schlesinger, Kyli Fitt, Kyo Hashimoto, Kyoko Kunoh, Kyoko Kurashima, Kyoko Shimoda, Kyung kyu Cho, La Tienda, Lalya Gaye, Lambert Kamps, Lara de Greef, Larisa Rezun Larry Barrow, Lars Fuhre, Lars Herzig, Lars Kynde, Lars Uwe Bleher, László Tamás, LAT 1:1, Laura Hernández, Laura Leiner, Laura Osorno, Laura Perin, Laura Weil, Laura Williams, Lauren Soloff, Laurence Makler, Laurent Déveze, Lavrans Lovlie, Layla Walter, Lázló Gergely, Leandro Madrazo, Leanne Rule, Leanne Shedlevski, Lara Verle, Lendzinskis, Lenka Kremenova, Leo Felipe, Leon Rost, Leon van Nistelroy, Leon van Spijk, Leonardo Murmora, lepe & the Kitchen Team Berlin, LeRoy Howard, Levien Nordeman, Li Nai Han, Li Shaobo, Li Tao, Li Xiao Dong, Liam Fitzgerald, Liana Chang, Liang Jingyu, Liesbeth de Jonge Life Bean, Lilienberg Sándor, Lin Jing, Lin Lin, Lin Wen Xuan, Lina Ozerkina, Linda Florence, Linda Krumina, Linda Watson, Lindsey Whitelaw, Linek Slabbekoorn, Liniers, Lisa Cahill, Liu Ding, Liu Hanxin, Liz Birkbeck, Liz Lambert, Lizan Freijsen, Lizzie Delfs, LN Boul, Loes ten Anscher, Loic Gestin, Lok Lau Lollipops, London Pecha Kucha Report, Lorenzo Bassano, Lori Wong, Lörincz Réka, LOTS, Lou Gilbert Scott, Lou Weis, Louis Jones, Louise Harpman, Love in my Velocity, Lowmind, Luc Monsigny, Luca Cuzzolin, Luca Nichetto, Luca Racchini, Luca Stasi, Lucie Kavánová, Lucinda Mason, Lucinda Noble, Luc Johnston, Lucy Musgrave, Luis Borrero, Luis Pereira Miguel, Luisa Bocchietto, Luka Hinse, Lukás Brom, Luke Chandresinghe, Luke Duncalfe, Luke Norris Luke Pearson, Luuk Bode, Luz Fernández Valderrama, LWL, Lykle de Vries , M K Raghavendra, Maarten Baas, Maartje Dijkstra, Maartje Lammers, Mads Mads Hjortefa, Magali Menant, Magne M Wiggen, Magnus Engström, Magnus Marsdal, Mai Itoh, Maja Gehrig, Maja Hawlina, Maki, Makoto Aida, Makoto Azuma, Makoto Hashimoto, Makoto Takei, Makoto Tanijiri, Makoto Tojiki, Malcolm Fraser, Mamoru Naito, Manabu Chiba, Manabu Naya, Manami, Manaub Manaub, Mannikitsch, Manon Vincent, Manuel de Rivero , Manuel Jiménez Navarro, Manuel Martí, Manuel Ocaña, Manuel Tardits, Manzanazeta, Mad Harada, Mapa Teatro, Marc Brinkmeyer, Marc Maurer, Marc Mazzarelli, Marc McQuade, Marc Neelen, Marc Pally, Marc Simmons, Marc Teer, Marc Wesseling Marc-André Plasse, Marcel Schobel, Marcel van der Pol , Marcela Steinbachová, Marcelo Ferla, Marcelo Guidoux Kalil, Marcelo Nunes, Marcelo Träsel, Marc Bertoldo, Marco Romanelli, Marco Zuttioni, Marcos Davidson, Marcus Fairs, Marcus Piper, Mardis Bagley, Mareike Reuch, Marek Adamov, Marek Pistora Marek Stepán, Margaret Griffin, Margarita Flores, Margit Greinoker, Margo Selby, Mari Becker, Mari Dutra, Mari Fiorelli, Mari Funaki, Mari Relander, Mar Sawada, Mari Xavier, Maria Jacobsson, Maria Mortati, Mariana Somma, Marianne Roosa, Mariano Toledo, Marie Delon, Marie Theres Deutsch, Marieke van der Weiden, Mariëtte Verschoor, Marije van de Vall, Marije Van Lidth de Jeude, Marijn Schenk, Mariko Enomoto, Mariko Yabe, Marine Peyre, Mario Feliciano Mario Minale, Marissa Looby, Marius Watz, Mark Brickey, Mark Dytham, Mark Glusker, Mark Hoekstra, Mark Holmes , Mark Janssen, Mark Majdanski, Mar Rolston, Mark Scott, Mark Shepard, Mark Simpson, Mark Veldman, Markéta Smrcková, Marko Ahtisaari, Markus Beckedahl, Markus Hofko, Markus Kison Markus Neckar, Markus Pretnar, Marlo Trejos, Maroussia Lévesque, Maróy Ákos, Marta de Menezes, Marta Pelegrín, Mårten Claesson, Marten de Jong Martijn van Diel, Martin Bricelj, Martín Churba, Martín Corujo, Martin Flatz, Martin Gsteiger, Martin Hrdina, Martin Jancok, Martin Jørgensen, Martin Krammer, Martin Putto, Martin Rajnis, Martin Relander, Martin Roeldolf, Martin Sawtell, Martin Wisniowsk, Martine Leroi, Marton Danoczy, Martti Kalliala Mary Jane Finlayson, Mary Lee Sjonell, Mary Ping, Maryanne Thompson, Masaaki Kato, Masaaki Takahashi, Masafumi Arita, Masahio Oie, Masahiro Harada Masaki Higuchi, Masaki Imamura, Masaki Kagajo, Masaki Yokokawa, Masako Ban, Masamichi Toyama, Masanobu Sugatsuke, Masanobu Takeishi, Masao Koizumi, Masashi Sogabe, Masatoshi Matsuzaki, Masaya Oonuki, Masaya Yamamoto, Massimo Bertolano, Masuzu Sawa, Matej Andraz Vogrincic, Mate Matias Ahrberg, Matilda Lindvall, Matt Biddulph, Matt H. , Matt Hume, Matt Rouse, Matt Smith, Matteo Gostanzo, Matth

Herbert, Matthew Kennedy, Matthew Manon, Matthew Taylor, Matthew Waltman, Matthias Kispert, Matthias Megyeri, Matthew Joscelyne, Mattia Nilsson, Mattijs van 't Hoff, Mauricio Bolivar, Mauricio Herrera, Mauricio Limón, Mauricio Marcín, Mauricio Melchor, Maurico Wainrot, Max Chen, Max Lamb, Max Zimmerman, Maxim Velcovsky, Mayor David Miller, Mayumi Ito, Mayumi Takahashi, Maziar Raein, Megan Baynes, Megan Rule, Meghan Novak, Mel Young, Melanie Taylor, Memo Delgado, Merijn Tinga, Merijn Tinga, Mette Ramsgaard Thomsen, Michael Carroll, Michael Chua, Michael Eddy, Michael Faulkner, Michael Johnson, Michael Kozel, Michael Kubo, Michael Landes, Michael Marriott, Michael McDaniel, Michael Pinto, Michael Schragger, Michael Several, Michael Sheetal, Michael Wallraff, Michaela Vieser, Michal Cimala, Michal Franek, Michal Kuzemensky, Michel van Wijk, Michele Senesi, Michelle Litvin, Michelle Qiao, Michiel Riedijk, Michiel Voet, Michiko Okano, Mie Yoon, Miha Artnak, Miha Horvat, Mihiro Yamamoto, Miho Masuzawa, Mikael Franzen, Mikan Gumi, Mike & Maaike, Mike Bordinaro, Mike Clark, Mike Faulkner, Mike Horne, Mike Kubeck, Mike Mills, Mike Reed, Mike Serafin, Mikelis Putrams, Mikiko Endo, Mikko Heikkinen, Mikko Laakkonen, Mikko Paakkanen, Milan Houser, Milan Malík, Milton Colonett, Mimi Hoang, Mimi Tong, Mina Sidi Ali, Mina Zabinkar, minm++, Mini-mal, Minke Themans, Minke Weeda, Minna Lukander, Miquel Adrià, Miranda Veljacic, Miriam Mlecek, Miriam Reeders, Mirjam Oosterbaan, Mirko.FM, Mischka Bartels, Mitsuaki Ando, Mitsue Hayasaka, Mitsuru Hamada, Mitya Kushelevic, Miyuki Nakahara, Modern Style in East asia 2004, Mohamed Sharif, Mohit Jayal, Molim, Momoyo Kaijima, Mondao Corp, Mondongo, Mónica Naranjo, Moov, Morag Myerscough, Morgan Fisher, Moriko Kira, Moritz Waldemeyer, Morten Lund, Motoaki Odani, Motoshi Chikamori, Mount Fuji Architects, Muf, Muid Latiff, Munetera Ujino, Musa, Muszbek Johanna, Muungano, Myeong-hee lee, Myra Ganong-Varadi, Nacho Martín, Nadine Roos, Nagisa Kldosaki, Nagy Csaba, Nagy Zsolt, Nahoko Wada, Naja, Naja Band, Naked Tokyo Collective, Namaiki, NanaAkua, Nanami Klein, Nanne de Ru, Nao Hirota, Naoki Ito, Naoki Terada, Naoko Kawano, Naomi Shedlevski, Naoya Kawabe, Naoya Kikuchi, Napangsiri Wanpen, Narayani Gupta, Narda Lepes, Nasa, Nat Hagey, Nat Soti, Natalie, Natalie Banaszak, Natalie Butts, Natalie Hunter, Nathan Shedroff, Nattavut Luenthaisong, Naya Manabu, NayaArata, Neale McGoldric, Neelam Chhiber, Neil Wallace, Nelleke Wegdam, Nelson Hyde, Netti Page, Neville Brody, Neville Mars, New Three Brothers, newsnewsnews, NEZ, Nez Loco Architects, Nial O conner, Nic Clear, Nicholas Eagles, Nichole Towler, Nick Barham, Nick Bauch, Nick Bell, Nick Hatfull, Nick Hoggett, Nick Johnson, Nick Luscombe, Nick Stedman, Nicklas Hultman, Nicola Pennington, Nicolai Krugar, Nicole Lecht, Niels Post, Niels Smits van Burgst, Nienke Wulp, Nigel Coates, Nigel Edginton, Nik Roope, Nik Schulz, Nika Zupanc, Nikki Butenschön, Nikolai Roth, Nils Poorman, Nimrod Weis, Nina Belk, Nina Gorfer, Nina Speyer, Ninan Joseph, Ninja, Nipa Doshi, Niszler Kata, No Para Innita, Nobara Catalina Hayakawa, Nobuhiro Tsukada, Nobuo Araki, Nobuto Fukutsu, Nobuyuki Nomura, Noh Workshop, Nontawat Numbenchapol, Nooka, Nora Lezano, NoricoKatayama, Noriko, Noriko Kanzawa, Noriyuki Otsuka, Noriyuki Tajima, Nynke Schaaf, Oak Tylor Smith, Oded Ezer, Oh-sang Kwon, Oki Unno, Ola Rune, Olaf Stevens, Olaf Martin hle, Oligatega Numeric, Oliver DiCicco, Oliver Domeisen, Oliver Hess, Oliver Kratzer, Oliver Langbein, Oliver Salway, Oliver Schutte, Oliver Wilm, Olivia Hyde, Olivier Fröhlich, Olivier Santoni-Costantini, Olivier Thereaux, Olman Orozco, Olof Persson, Olympia Kazi, Omar Khan, Omar Rodriguez-Graham, Omega Group, Ona Vinyamata Tubella, Onno Donkers, Oonagh O'Hagan, Oooke Makoto, openTop, Osami, Osamu Nishida, Oscar Barranco, Oscar Brahim, Otakar Dusek, Oysten Austad, P. Simon Ostan, Pablo Altclas, Pablo Sendra, Pablo Sotomayor, palla, Pang Khee Teik, Pantea Tehrani, Paola Suhonen, Paolo Tassinari, Parag Sharma, Parinya Pichetsiriporn, parisydneytokyo.com, Pascal Dowers, Patricia Fernández Fernández, Patricia Schraven, Patrick Corrigan, Patrick Kruithof, Patrick Lynch, Patrick Matzenbacher, Patrick Meagher, Patrick Norguet, Patrick Oancia, Patrick Reynolds, Patrik Fredrikson, Pattern, Patty Lundeen, Paul Aragon, Paul Barbera, Paul Baron, Paul Bennun, Paul Duffy, Paul Fuog, Paul Gelinas, Paul Gonzalez, Paul Heritage, Paul Jamtgaard, Paul Leroy, Paul McAneary, Paul Priestman, Paul Reed, Paul Smith, Paul Sutcliffe, Paul Vanouse, Paul Vinken, Paula Kagan, Paulett Singley, Paulina Lasa, Paulo Scott, Pawalee Chirakranont, Pax Chimera, Payam Sharifi, Payamédicos, Peat Duggins, Pecha Kucha Copenhagen, Pedrita Peeple, Peeraphat Kittisuwat, Peikwen Cheng, Pekka Harni, Penny Modra, Perinne Vigneron, Pernilla Cederberg, Pernilla Klüft, Pete Burgy, Peter Anderson, Peter Ayres, Peter Bootsma, Peter C. Krell, Peter Cachola Schmal, Peter de Kan, Peter de Ruiter, Peter Exley, Peter Hallén, Peter Harding, Peter Jamtgarro, Péter Klobusovszki, Peter Krech, Peter Liversedge, Peter Nyboer, Peter Poulet, Péter Pozsár, Peter Rummel, Peter Sandhaus, Peter Simensky, Peter Vosper, Petr Babák, Petr Suske, Petra Eichler, Petra Jenning, Petteri Kolinen, Phelim McDermott, Phil Ayres, Phil Fish, Phil Lubliner, Philip Smith, Philip Wood, Phil Worthington, Phillip Fung, Phillip Obayda, Phillip Wood, Philomena Keet, Phoebe Dakin, Phoebe Jan, Phuong-nam Nguyen, Piero Faraguna, Piero Zucch, Pierre Henniquant, Pietro Valle, Pina Petricone, ping pong design, Plan V, Platoon, Plazes, Please hold this cake, PLUS DJs, Pollyanna Whitman, Pongto Wachirapoka, Popular de lujo, Pozna Anita, Prachya Pinkaew, Pradhana Chariyavilaskul, Preston Zly, Prima Chakrabandhu Na Ayudhya, Productora, Projektil architek, Prostoroz in Kombinat, Przemek Sobocki, Punkah, Quentin Newark, Quicksand, R. Ferrari, Rachel Allen, Rachel Codling Asian Culture Organize, Radames, Radio Capsula, Rafael García Tenorio, Rafael Iglesia, Rafael Puyana, Raffael Graf, Rageh Omaar, Raina Kumra, Raj Liberhan, Rajesh Thind, Rajiv Sethi, Ralf Anderl, Ralf Grauel, Ralf Pasel, Ralf Steeg, Rally Conurbano, Ramon Knoester, Ramon Pruisscher, Randal Marsh, Randolph Langenbach, Raul Marroquin, Ravi Agarwal, Ravi Kalia, RE, Rebeca Mendez, Regan Gentry, Regan Gentry, Regina Loukotová, Reiko Yamaguchi, Rein Bish, Rein de Vries, Reinhard Reitzenstein, Rejah Bahk, Rena Watami, Renae Tapley, Renan Schmidt, Renato A Pirotta, Rene Boonstra, René Boonstra, Rene Brazel, Renee Petropolous, Re-plus Inc, Reto Wettach, Revista Colectiva, Rhona Wood, Rhydian Phillips, rh design, Ricardo Levinton, Richard Goodwin, Richard Kegler, Richard Koek, Richard, Richard Nylon, Richie Tanaka, Rick Miller, Rick Miller, Rick Pearson, Rickard Lindqvist, RieIsono, Ries Strave, Riharb Eunts, Risto Kuulasmaa, Ristomatti Ratia, Rita Godlevski, Rita Marni, Ritsert Inia, River Kuo, Rob Kidney, Rob Manuel, Rob Rainbow, Rob